The Life and Times of

ROGER CASEMENT

ROGER CASEMENT.

The Life and Times of
ROGER CASEMENT

BY

HERBERT O. MACKEY

DUBLIN
C. J. FALLON LIMITED
1954

First published, December, 1954

PUBLISHED BY C. J. FALLON LTD, 43 PARKGATE ST, DUBLIN, AND PRINTED IN
THE REPUBLIC OF IRELAND BY CAHILL & CO. LTD, PARKGATE PRINTING
WORKS, DUBLIN

PREFACE

THE AIM of the writer, throughout the following pages, has been to present a true picture of Casement—the man, his life, and his work. The facts have been culled from reliable sources. Original letters, documents, and contemporary records have been studied as well as the standard works and references, a bibliography of which will be found at the end of the book.

Copious extracts from Casement's letters and writings as well as his speech from the dock are given, so as to enable the reader, while making use of the information herein afforded, also, independently, to judge for himself what we set before him.

The writer is deeply indebted to the late Mrs. Gertrude Parry for much valuable material, to Miss Ada MacNeill, to Dr. Patrick MacCartan and to Dr. Hayes McCoy of the National Museum, for their assistance and encouragement. A debt of gratitude is also due to Dr. Richard Hayes, Director of the National Library, to Dr. McLysaght of the Manuscript section, and to the assistant librarians and staff for their unfailing kindness and courtesy.

HERBERT O. MACKEY, *F.R.C.S.*

39 FITZWILLIAM SQUARE,
   DUBLIN
10th November, 1954

CONTENTS

LIST OF ILLUSTRATIONS

INTRODUCTION

A DISTINGUISHED English judge, Sir Thomas A. Jones, K.C., who had been, when a young barrister, assigned as junior counsel in the trial of Roger Casement, writing many years after the trial, said: —

Behind the trial, of course, loomed the shadow of the tragedy of the Anglo-Irish problem. . . . It is impossible to form an unbiassed judgment on the pitiful tragedy of Casement's end on the scaffold unless it is related to the still more pitiful tragedy of the relations between Great Britain and Ireland.

When one nation by the accidental reason of a numerical majority absorbs a neighbouring nation numerically less, and the greater speaks a different language and springs from a different tribe and then imposes its laws upon the subjugated people, the position creates a cruel conflict of loyalties and exposes the citizens of the smaller state inevitably to the awful penalties of treason. When such conquest becomes complete in course of time, the loyal citizen of the smaller state must, from the standpoint of the legalist, desert his own countrymen and betray his own tribe to its enemies in order to avoid the hangman's rope which is in the hands of his rulers. Treason, then, is no longer what it started as, namely, a man's betrayal of his tribe; it has become a perversion of the original crime, since loyalty to the larger state must involve betrayal of his own people. . . . It is also none the less true that a plot to subvert the authority of the state is not treason so long as the plotters are successful.

Casement returned to his native land in 1913, when Sir Edward Carson and Mr. F. E. Smith (as he then was) had formed the Ulster Army, the army that was to defy the British Government by an appeal to force in the event of Home Rule. This coincidence of his return to Ireland with the preparation for semi-rebellion in Ulster set his feet on the path that eventually led to the scaffold. . . . Casement had imbibed the spirit and the sentiment of Irish Nationalism in his boyhood. In 1904, he had identified himself with the Gaelic League, and he had contributed articles to journals which advocated the recognition of Ireland's separate nationhood, the revival of her language and the cultivation of her ancient literature. It is not difficult to comprehend the reaction produced in Casement's mind by the political situation in Ireland when he returned home in 1913—the drilling and the army of Ulster, and the complete absence of any kind of attempt on the part of the British Government to suppress the incipient rebellion. The formation of the Irish National Volunteers in response to the challenge from Carson's army in Ulster followed as a matter of course, and into this Casement flung himself with as much ardour as Carson or Smith had flung themselves into the Ulster movement. . . . The turning point was reached when the Liberal Government decided to suspend the operation of the Home Rule Act on the outbreak of the war. . . . Irish Nationalists viewed with disgust and dismay this abject surrender to the threat of armed force from Ulster. . . . ' Sold again ' and ' England has broken her word once more ' and the ' Betrayal of Home Rule ' . . . . noted the feeling among the rank and file of the Nationalists. Efforts had been made to obtain assistance from Germany by the Ulster leaders with such expressions as : ' Mausers or Kaisers and any King you like.' How far these Ulster leaders had gone in the direction of getting other things besides mauser rifles from Germany will not be known till the secret political memoirs of those times are published. At all periods . . . . the complete truth about these matters does not become known for a generation or two. Some light has been shed by the disclosures in a recent biography of the late Sir Austen Chamberlain.

The political antecedents of the attorney-general (Smith) who had been as prominent as the late Lord Carson in the semi-rebellion in Ulster, in 1913, were notorious.

' Carson figured as attorney-general (with a salary of £7,000 and fees) to be replaced presently by his associate in the Ulster sedition, F. E. Smith. Grosser insult was never offered to a friendly people. Casement was tried and executed for treason but his prosecutor was Sir F. E. Smith, of the Ulster insurrection—a shocking conjunction.

' *H. G. Wells.'*

Casement was a tall, handsome man, his black hair and his black beard giving a marked distinction to his finely cut features. It was impossible to listen to his clear, low, well-modulated voice, without realising that he was . . . . an able and cultivated man. The quality of mind which most impressed the writer was his sincerity and his intellectual integrity. At the last interview at Pentonville, Casement wore the prison garb of a convict with a broad arrow. He sat at (the head of) a table, armed warders on each side, with junior counsel and solicitor at the other end. His demeanour then was the same as at the other interviews—dignified, courteous and restrained. He expressed at the end his thanks for the efforts his lawyers had made on his behalf. He smiled—rather sadly as I thought—as he bade us good-bye.

The case presented to the jury for the crown was founded upon the ancient Act of Edward III, passed in 1351. The text was in Norman-French and the English versions published in different text books varied in punctuation. The actual words of the Act of 1351 are, literally translated:

'If a man be adherent to the King's enemies in his realm giving to them aid and comfort in the realm or elsewhere'.

The prosecuting attorney claimed that the words 'giving them aid and comfort in the realm' should be read as though they were contained in a parenthesis, and the words 'or elsewhere' related to the words 'adherent to the King's enemies'. The defence relied on the words as they stood and as they were written, i.e. without punctuation.

A visit paid by the writer to the Record Office, where he examined the original membranes on which the text is written, made it quite clear that Parliament had employed the words with neither parenthesis nor punctuation marks at all.

The appeal that Casement made to the Irish soldiers was to join an Irish brigade, which was to fight not for Germany but for Ireland's independence. Most of the soldiers who were called upon at the trial to give their recollections of Casement's speech to them agreed that Casement had said they were to fight for Ireland only when Germany, after winning a battle at sea, would land the Irish Brigade in Ireland.

Casement declared in his first speech to the court:

'First,' he said, 'I never at any time advised Irishmen to fight for Turks against Russians nor to fight with Germans on the western front. Secondly, I never asked an Irishman to fight for Germany. I have always claimed that he has no right to fight for any land but Ireland.'

With equal brevity he dismissed scornfully the reference made by the Attorney-General to his pension.

' As to my pension and the honour of knighthood conferred on me, I will say one word only. The pension I had earned by services rendered and it was assigned by law. The knighthood it was not in my power to refuse.'

He went on : —

' There is a widespread imputation of German gold. I owe it to those in Ireland who are assailed with me on this very ground to nail the lie once and for all. . . . Those who know me know the incredibility of this malicious invention, for they know from my past record that I have never sold myself to any man or to any Government, and have never allowed any Government to use me. From the moment I landed on the Continent until I came home again to Ireland, I never asked for nor accepted a single penny of foreign money, neither for myself, nor for any Irish cause, nor for any purposes whatsoever. I refute so obvious a slander. Money was offered to me in Germany more than once, and offered liberally and unconditionally, but I rejected every suggestion of this kind, and I left Germany a poorer man than I entered it. . . .'

The theme of his speech was the unhappy fate of every small nation in being held in the grip of those conflicting loyalties which are inherent in the everlasting iniquity of racial conquest and annexation. To him, loyalty to Ireland and not to England was the supreme duty of the Irishman, even though it meant his death. He compressed the essence of the tragic problem into a single, pregnant sentence : —

' If small nationalities were to be the pawns in the game of embattled giants, I saw no reason why Ireland should shed her blood in any cause but her own; and if that be treason beyond the seas, I am not ashamed to avow it or to answer for it here with my life.'

In the history of civilisation, the chief characteristic of the Great War as compared with previous calamities will be seen to be the growth of the modern science of calumny (or propaganda) as a weapon in the armoury of belligerent nations. No one can read the European press to-day without realising the awful power wielded by the printed word in the destruction of moral judgment. What the verdict of history may be, no one save a seer can foretell

—the flight of time is inexorable and the merciful hands of oblivion are always at work. Fortunately, the great speech of Sir Roger Casement before sentence remains in the records of the law. It will be read by his fellow Irishmen generations after his judges, his prosecutors, his lawyers and his calumniators have long been forgotten.

'. . . . Ireland has seen her sons—aye, and her daughters, too—suffer from generation to generation always for the same cause, meeting always the same fate, and always at the hands of the same power; and always a fresh generation has passed on to withstand the same oppression. . . .

' The cause that begets this indomitable persistency, the faculty of preserving through centuries of misery the remembrance of lost liberty, this, surely, is the noblest cause men ever strove for, ever lived for, ever died for. If this be the cause I stand here to-day indicted for and convicted of sustaining, then I stand in a goodly company and a right noble succession.'

—ROGER CASEMENT.
(*Speech from the dock.*)

CHAPTER I

EARLY YEARS AND AFRICAN ADVENTURE

ROGER DAVID CASEMENT was born on 1st September, 1864, at Lawson Terrace, Sandycove, County Dublin. Following the death of his mother in 1873, his father having died a few years previously, young Casement was sent to stay with his uncle at Magherintemple, Ballycastle, County Antrim. His father, also Roger Casement, of Magherintemple House, Ballycastle, County Antrim, a captain in the 3rd Dragoon Guards and later captain in the County Antrim Militia, had strong nationalist leanings and resigned his commission rather than take part in the eviction and destruction of the houses of the peasantry in County Sligo. He joined with John Mitchel, the Irish patriot, in the movement for the liberation of Ireland and when Mitchel was captured, sentenced to penal servitude for life and sent to the penal prison in Van Diemen's Land, Casement was exiled. He fought under Louis Kossuth in the war of Hungarian Independence and later lived for some time in Paris, where he met and married a Catholic young lady, Miss Anne Jephson, a native of County Wexford. They later returned to Ireland where Roger David Casement was born in 1864.

Soon after his ninth birthday young Casement was sent to the Ballymena Academy where he remained until his seventeenth year, spending his holidays at Magherintemple. The library in his uncle's house was well stocked with books on Ireland and Irish history and there he spent many leisure hours acquiring that knowledge of his country; its ancient glories and the centuries of cruel oppression; the many rebellions crushed with ruthless savagery; the dread period of penal days, and finally, the 1798 period when his countrymen of every creed were massacred with unexampled ferocity by the English troops and mercenaries.

He then formed a resolution which was to remain with him all his life:— to endeavour to free Ireland from the English yoke.

In 1881 he took up an appointment with the Elder Dempster Shipping Company, of which his uncle was a director, and re-

mained for two years at this post in the Liverpool offices of the
Company.

Young Casement with the spirit of adventure which was to lead
him to the accomplishment of such great work for humanity in
later life, set sail in 1883 for the West Coast of Africa in one of
the Company's ships. Four years later, having acquired an extensive
knowledge of West Africa and the Congo, he joined an expedition
organised by the American General, Henry Sandford. The object
of the expedition was the exploration of the Congo, and with his
special knowledge Casement was a great acquisition to the party.
When this important work had been carried out the discoveries
made by the explorers became the subject of an extensive lecturing
tour in the United States. One of the results of this tour was that
his reputation as an explorer and administrator became firmly established, and he soon came to be recognised as one of the very few
men who had a thorough and first-hand knowledge of Central
Africa.

In 1892 he was appointed a travelling commissioner in the service
of the Niger Coast Protectorate, a post which he filled with distinction, and at the end of his term he was rewarded with official
commendation for his services. Leaving Nigeria in 1895 he was
appointed Consul at Lourenço Marques. Here he remained for
three years, when in July, 1898, he was made Consul for the
Portuguese Possessions in West Africa south of the Gulf of Guinea.
His residence was at Loanda. While there he also carried out the
duties of Consul in the Gaboon and Consul to the Independent
State of the Congo.

It is of interest to note that in these early days Ireland and its
problems were uppermost in his mind, and his letters home usually
contained requests for Irish newspapers and for full information
on Irish affairs.

When the Boer War broke out, Casement, who had from
Lourenço Marques learned much of the local affairs in Swaziland,
was sent on a special mission to Capetown. From Capetown in
1900 he returned to the Congo as Consul at Kinchasa in the Congo
State. In July, 1901, he was given the additional post of Consul
for the French Congo Colony. For three more years he was engaged
in these responsible positions, and the experience which he gained
served as the prelude to and prepared him for his later work of
investigation into the administration and trading conditions in the
Congo.

CHAPTER II

THE CONGO HORROR

It was on the 5th of June, 1903, that he left Matadi for Leopold-ville to commence this investigation which was to last two and a half months, and entailed travelling through hundreds of miles of jungle and swamp and large areas ravaged with sleeping sickness, yellow fever, and smallpox. This journey in tropical heat and in high summer took a heavy toll of his strength, and the experiences and almost incredible brutalities which he witnessed and about which he made full and detailed reports must have made an indelible impression on one whose mind was filled with a hatred of cruelty, injustice and oppression.

He was, however, well equipped for this enterprise being possessed of a thorough knowledge of Central Africa and endowed with indomitable courage and determination. In one of such a kindly nature and warmness of heart, nothing but his inflexible will could enable him to endure, over these months, the daily sight of the cruel suffering, mutilations and savage torture inflicted on the native population.

Throughout his life he had always been the friend of suffering humanity and of oppressed peoples everywhere, no matter to what race, religion, or nationality they belonged. His dominating impulse was to champion the oppressed, and wherever he went he never relaxed in his fervent devotion to his own country. This is evident from his letters, e.g. : —

' There is so much to be done in the Congo matter that we shall need all our strength and the support of every friend of the weak and oppressed to help those poor persecuted beings in Central Africa. It is a tyranny beyond conception—save only, perhaps, to an Irish mind alive to the horrors once daily enacted in this land.

' I think it must have been my insight into human suffering and into the ways of the spoiler and the ruffian who takes " civilisation " for his watchword when his object is the appropriation of the land and labour of others for his personal profit, and which the tale of

English occupation in Ireland so continually illustrates, that gave me the deep interest I felt in the lot of the Congo natives.

' Every argument by which King Leopold and his aiders seek to justify the merciless oppression of the Central African today was stereotyped in the " laws " and measures of the past in this country. We had it all: even to " moral and material regeneration." '

During his stay at Leopoldville he observed closely the provision made there for the natives and was particularly revolted by the state of affairs in the native hospital. A quotation from his report reads:

' When I visited the three mud huts which serve this purpose, all of them dilapidated, and two of them with the thatched roofs almost gone, I found seventeen sleeping-sickness patients, male and female, lying about in the utmost dirt. Most of them were lying on the bare ground, several on the pathway in front of the houses, and one, a woman, had fallen into the fire just prior to my arrival (while in the final insensible stage of the disease), and had burned herself badly. She had since been well bandaged, but was still lying out on the ground with her head almost in the fire and while I sought to speak to her, in turning, she upset a pot of scalding water over her shoulder. All of the seventeen persons I saw were near the end, and on my second visit, two days later, the 19th June, I found one of them lying dead out in the open.'

Leaving Leopoldville on the 2nd July he reached a village 160 miles away which he had known in 1887 and found that the population had fallen from 5,000 to 500. Here he found that the practice was to send out armed expeditions among the natives for the purpose of forcing them to bring in their goats and fowl. Writing of one such expedition he said:

' The result of this expedition . . . . was that in fourteen small villages traversed, seventeen persons disappeared. Sixteen of these whose names were given to me were killed by the soldiers, and their bodies recovered by their friends, and one was reported missing. Of those killed eleven were men, three women, and one, a boy of five years. Ten persons were tied up and taken away as prisoners, but were released on payment of sixteen goats by their friends, except one, a child, who died at Bolobo.'

At Bolobo Casement was delayed for ten days awaiting a steamer, and there, too, he saw that the system of compulsory labour was a cruel burden on the natives. A journey of a further twenty miles revealed even worse cases of savagery practised by the white administrators. Here the natives were sent out to get rubber and if they failed to bring in enough to satisfy their white masters an official would line them up one behind the other and shoot them thus, all with the one bullet. In addition to this system of terror the living conditions of the natives were appalling and the collecting and noting of these barbarities must have been a revolting and nauseating experience.

Later, when back in Ireland, he wrote:

' There is so much to do here in Ireland that sometimes my heart faints when I think of the Congo and all its claims upon me, but I cannot, even for the sake of my own dear country, forsake the poor people out there.

' And that is the way, I am sure, the claim of the Congo people must appeal to every sincere and genuine Irish native: the more we love our land and wish to help our people the more keenly we feel we cannot turn a deaf ear to suffering and injustice in any part of the world.

' I am quite sure that if I had not been an Irishman and an ardent believer in the nationality and rights of Ireland I should have passed thro' those scenes of Congo suffering humanity with a cold, or at any rate so reserved a heart, that I should never have committed myself as I did to assume an attitude of insistence so uncompromising that the doubts of my chiefs were swept away and they permitted my report to see publicity . . . the dastardly cowardice of the whole vile business out there would make you burn with the resentment I feel at it, but since I cannot speak to you with my lips I have tried to talk straight with my pen.'

In a steam launch on the 23rd July, he left Bolobo, calling at several villages on the way, on the French side of the river, and later reached Lukolela. After two days here where he found that the natives were exploited in the same inhuman manner and as a result that the population had dropped from 5,000 to 600, Casement moved on to a place which had in 1887, the date of his previous visit, a population of 4,000 to 5,000. This village he now discovered had completely disappeared and a camp was set up there in which a large number of particularly savage black men were recruited and drilled under white officers. This irregular army was called ' Force Publique'. When out on punitive expeditions against the native population fearful barbarities were committed. Casement wrote:

' During the course of these operations there had been much loss of life, accompanied, I fear, by a somewhat general mutilation of the dead, as proof that the soldiers had done their duty.'

Terror of the white man was particularly noticeable in the Upper Congo, for when Casement entered one village the inhabitants fled to the woods taking their possessions with them. Among the accounts of the frightful atrocities perpetrated by the soldiery was one where they had killed the natives in great numbers, cut off their hands and collected these in baskets to take to the white man. He counted the collection—200 in all.

In the Lake Mantumba district Casement saw numbers of the natives who were mutilated by having their hands cut off. Of one boy so mutilated, aged twelve, Casement said:

' His father and mother were killed beside him. He saw them killed and a bullet hit him as he fell. He here showed me a deep cicatrised scar at the back of his head, just at the nape of the neck, and said it was there the bullet had struck him. He fell down, presumably insensible, but came to his senses while his hand was being hacked off at the wrist. I asked him how it was he could possibly lie silent and give no sign. He answered that he felt the cutting, but was afraid to move, knowing that he would be killed if he showed any sign of life.' For this unfortunate boy Casement took measures to provide help.

This deliberate mutilation of human beings was particularly harrowing to Casement's feelings and he says:

' It was not a native custom prior to the coming of the white man . . . . it was the deliberate act of the soldiers of the European administration, and these men never made any concealment that in committing these acts they were but obeying the positive orders of their superiors.'

Continuing his journey from Lake Mantumba he arrived at Coquilhatville. Here he spent five days and the levies, forced labour, and punitive expeditions had greatly depopulated the district. In one village twenty-five men were seized by the soldiery and nothing was heard of them afterwards. In addition a fine of 2,750 francs was imposed, a sum which, of course, could not be raised, and so the unfortunate natives were forced to sell their wives and children to pay the amount.

The rivers Lopori and the Maringa, which are each about 350 miles long, unite at the village of Bassankusa to form the river Lulongo. A concession known as the A.B.I.R. was located in this region and employed a large body of forest sentinels who were spread out among the villages whom they terrorised in a most shameful manner. Here the soldiery were given a counted number of cartridges when setting out on a punitive expedition with the order to each that:

'He must bring back every one not used: and for every one used he must bring back a right hand.'

Going further up the Lulongo River he decided to make a surprise visit to a village in an out-of-the-way region. He was shocked to find two sentries guarding fifteen women. Of these five were nursing their infants while three others were expectant mothers. Mistaking Casement for a 'missionary', one of the guards explained that the women had been rounded up in order to force their husbands to bring in a quantity of rubber. Casement was enquiring why they held the women 'because it was the men who collected the rubber', the man replied:

'Don't you see, if I caught and kept the men, who would work the rubber? But if I catch their wives, the husbands are anxious to have them home again, and so the rubber is brought in quickly up to the mark.' As night came on Casement saw that these fifteen wretched women were tied together either ankle to ankle or neck to neck and so left until the morning.

Bongandanga, 130 miles up the Lopori river, was his next call, and here forced labour and the other iniquities were also only too evident. Leaving here on September 3rd, he commenced his return journey, but before he set out many of the local people came and brought with them, men, women, and children who were mutilated in a most revolting manner and they explained in detail to him the horrors of their savage treatment at the hands of the white administrators. But as time was pressing he had to leave for the first station of his return journey, and when he arrived there he was met by a crowd who showed him a boy of fifteen whose hand had been hacked off at the wrist and also had a bullet wound in his forearm.

He reached Coquilhatville on the 11th September and on the 15th arrived at Stanley Pool his point of departure. With as short a delay as possible he set out for London carrying the manuscript of all his investigations, with maps, notes and references. Arrived there he lost no time in preparing a comprehensive report which he completed on December 11th, 1903, and this he immediately handed to Lord Lansdowne, the Foreign Secretary.

About this time he founded the Congo Reform Association. He wrote:

'I don't want the Brussels gang of robbers to be able to say that the Congo Reform movement has been got up and engineered by Protestant missionaries. As a matter of fact it *originated* solely with me: I gave the idea to Morel whose generous heart and fiery soul at once responded—and our first recruit was as I say that good Irishman and good Catholic, Lord ffrench. When I asked him to help me by lending his name he said he could not refuse—that it was the duty of a Christian, of every Christian who believed in his faith in God, to help such a call.'

Confidently he wrote:

'The Commission will confirm my report "up to the hilt". That will be a triumph indeed—and a triumph for Ireland, too —as I may some day tell you. I knew well that if I told the truth about the devilish Congo conspiracy of robbers I should pay for it in my own future; but when I made up my mind to tell, at all costs, it was the image of my poor old country stood first before my eyes. The whole thing had been done once to her— down to every detail—she, too, had been " flung *reward* to human hounds "—and I felt that, an Irishman, come what might to myself, I should tell the whole truth. I burned my boats deliberately, and forced the F.O. either to repudiate me, or back my report. And yet I knew quite well, in the end, I should have to go overboard, and I wrote that on September 4, 1903, the day I wrote to the Governor General at Boma denouncing the whole infamous system, and so committing myself to " no compromise ".'

'It is a mistake,' he wrote, 'for an Irishman to mix himself up with the English. He is bound to do one of two things—either to go to the wall, if he remains Irish, or become an Englishman himself. You see I very nearly did become one once. At the Boer war time, I had been away from Ireland for years—out of touch with everything native to my heart and mind, trying hard to do my duty and every fresh act of duty made me appreciably nearer the ideal of the Englishman—altho' at heart, underneath all and unsuspected almost by myself I had remained an Irishman. Well, the war (the Boer War) gave me the qualms at the end—the concentration camps a bigger one—and finally when up in those lonely Congo forests where I found Leopold I found also myself—the incorrigible Irishman. I was remonstrated with there by British highly respectable and religious missionaries. " Why make such a bother," they said, " the State represents Law and Order and after all these people *are* savages and must be repressed with a firm hand ".'

' Every fresh discovery I made of the hellishness of the Leopold system threw me back on myself alone for guidance. I knew that the F.O. wouldn't understand the thing—or that if they did they would take no action, for I realised then that I was looking at the tragedy with the eyes of another race—of a people once hunted themselves, whose hearts were based on affection as the root principle of contact with their fellow men and whose estimate of life was not of something eternally to be appraised at its market "price". And I said to myself then, far up the Lulongo River, that I would do *my* part as an Irishman, wherever it might lead me to personally. Since that, each year has confirmed me in my faith in that point of view.'

The report was published in February and shortly afterwards, in view of its great importance, copies were sent to Rome, Madrid, Paris, Berlin, St. Petersburg, Vienna, The Hague, Copenhagen, Stockholm, Brussels, Lisbon, and Constantinople.

The report was published later in the form of a White Paper, and when circulated profoundly shocked the public conscience. World-wide attention was drawn to the iniquities of the Congo administration with its attendant brutalities and the savage treatment of the native population. A storm of protest was aroused by these disclosures, and Casement soon became a world-famous figure and justly earned an international reputation for the outstanding work he had carried out in the cause of humanity.

On the 30th June, 1905, he received the C.M.G. in recognition of his work. This decoration which made him a ' Commander of the Order of St. Michael and St. George ' embarrassed him considerably because it was an English honour which he in no way sought. In fact he never used the title and the parcel containing the insignia of the Order remained unopened.

His work which was crowned with success earned for him the gratitude of the whole world. The peoples of the Congo were freed from their cruel bondage: fair conditions were prescribed and justice secured for them by international action.

Chapter III

THE STRUGGLE FOR NATIONAL EXISTENCE

Casement with impaired health now returned to Ireland for a prolonged rest. During this time he became actively engaged in the Irish independence movement and took a great interest in the advancement of the Gaelic League and all that it stood for, viz., an Irish-speaking nation and the revival of the old traditional culture of the country.

Referring to the language revival he wrote:

' I got back to Ireland early in 1904—got to find the Gaelic League at once—and all the old hopes and longings of my boyhood have sprung to life again. What we are now fighting for in Ireland, more than anything else, is the continuity of our national character. If we do not preserve that (or restore it rather) we shall cease to be Irish. The language alone could not restore it. We must recapture many other things England, or contact with her, has filched from us. She has no appreciation of anything but success—success in marketable terms.

'Dr. O'Beirne (of Tawin) is cheering in the extreme. He wanted to go abroad and I begged him to face *all* things at home in Ireland, because she needed every son and he is facing the problem on the spot . . . . see what can be done to further help Tawin. I have £18 of their money still in hand—I'll make it £20 and send it to this committee of Tawin men—but they need some little outside advice and encouragement I feel sure. If you go to Galway this year do try and meet Seamus O'Beirne and visit Tawin and get an Craobhin to go there. His visit to Tawin and a Gaelic speech by him to them might make the whole peninsula, of which Tawin is only the jutting point, Irish speaking again.

' They *all* have the language—every household, but the majority are anglicised or being anglicised and laugh at their own pure tongue. Oh, how awful it is to think of. This casting off of their own forefathers' souls, this deliberate race suicide. The Japanese are conquering the East thro' faith in and veneration of their own past—

glorifying their dead fathers even to the point of worship and offering to *them* the victories their sons gain today. And here are we Irish with a past as ancient as the Japanese and a language going back to the dawn of the world rejecting the nobler life we are still in touch with. . . . I remember Hugh Law saying to me when I went to see Charles Russell, " The Congo is *urgent;* the case of Ireland is different, urgency doesn't matter so much there." Now when you come to think of it how entirely and dreadfully wrong Hugh Law was. Africa can wait—for centuries and centuries; she will still be Africa. The blackman will still be a blackman. Leopold might murder millions, but nothing could destroy or efface the ineffaceable negro, his ways, his colour, his mind, his stature and all that makes him the negro. No matter how cruel the persecution he might suffer the negro will remain unchanged and unchangeable and Africa could *always* be reconstituted by her own sons and the waves of European misgovernment ebbed back leaving no trace upon her shores or native character.

' In the case of Ireland—how different. Her case is desperate; it is now or never, indeed. Ireland can wait less than any other country in the world. If she is not helped now all the help of Christendom a few years hence cannot restore her as Ireland. It is a case of an ancient people and all that differentiated them from the other races being saved *now*, or of being lost for ever. Hugh Law, quite unconsciously, there spoke the mind of the Party—that is why I despair of them. They have substituted for Ireland their organisation. *It* can wait, of course. It is now in existence 30 years and an Irish Party might very credibly be in existence 30 years hence, repeating just the same *formulae* and attending just as regularly and honestly at Westminster—but there will be no Ireland. They do not realise that while they are talking in England the real Ireland is growing silent —and that silence now has the end well in sight.'

Regarding the Irish language he wrote :

' In 1904 I joined the Gaelic League. It was abundantly clear to my mind that the spoken language was dying fast, and that *it* was the one sole hope of the tongue of the Gael surviving as a spoken tongue. . . . . There is, as Dr. Hyde says, only the *seed* of Irish left. . . . . I tried six years ago or five years ago to get people in Ireland to see what Dr. H. says, and no one would respond. The Gaelic League thought that by chanting nouns and verbs in Dublin streets they would revive Irish as a spoken tongue—chopping turnips would revive it as well. The one and *only* thing was to keep it a *living* tongue, from mother to child there in its last home by the Irish peninsulas of the West and South-West.'

It was natural for an Irishman, who had been championing the rights of the oppressed peoples of the Congo, to see a parallel in his own land. The Irish nation he knew was oppressed and held down by England. He had succeeded in obtaining justice for another subject race and now he set about doing the same for his own people. The Irish, he plainly realised, were a nation rightly struggling to be free, and in a letter to an English friend in July, 1906, he wrote:

'You know my views well. If the British Empire is to endure it can only be by recognising Ireland's right, not by " holding down " a " sister country ". Every people has a right to live its own life, provided that it works thereby no grievous wrong on its neighbours. England has that right; but she has no right to insist that another country shall adopt her mode of life, and to break them on the wheel if they resist. . . . .'

He had a rooted dislike of Imperialism and the attitude of England towards Irish national aspirations he despised and rejected. This can be seen from his letters:

'I have no belief in Englishmen. Do you know what Michael Davitt wrote of them? : " The idea of being ruled by Englishmen is to me the chief agony of existence. They are a nation without faith, truth or conscience, enveloped in a panoplied pharisaism and an incurable hypocrisy. Their moral appetite is fed on falsehood. They profess Christianity and believe only in Mammon. They talk of Liberty while ruling India and Ireland against the principles of a Constitution professed as political faith but prostituted to the interests of class and landlord rule." (Michael Davitt to the Scotsman Davidson, 27 August, 1902).

'You remember Charles Peace, how he went to church and " prayed "—eminently respectable. Well, the English are a race of Charles Peaces—he is the true national type—a race of successful criminals—Charles Peace, well armed and ready to shoot at sight any of his hapless victims. The most successful are made Peers in order that the national succession of ideas may be preserved and the booty remain intact.'

CHAPTER IV

A MEMORABLE EXPLOIT

The following letter and the article illustrate the tradition in the Casement family of the love of freedom and the hatred of oppression :

24th February, 1905.

' There is an interesting article in this week's " United Irishman " about my father's ride across Hungary in 1849 to help Kossuth.

' I wrote the article myself. I am trying to get more facts of the actual ride to give a Hungarian friend who is writing an article for a party magazine on the subject. My father died when I was a very young boy—and I can only recall the fact of the ride itself, and Palmerston taking him by the arm after dinner and leading him round the room to show him pictures. Also the Russian patrol in the Carpathians.

' I do not want it commented on in English papers for it would not help poor Congo reform if I, the apostle of Congo reform, were to be now depicted as an arrant Irishman—and son of another. But I thought the story would do good in Ireland, and so I gave it very gladly to the " United Irishman ".'

This is the article which appeared in the ' United Irishman ' on 25th February, 1905, and signed ' X '.

Kossuth's Irish Courier.

There is an incident of the Hungarian struggle for national existence in 1849 which should have an especial interest for Irishmen—apart from the larger interest that great story of constancy and enlightened patriotism must always have for them. This incident is recorded by Kossuth, himself, in ' Meine Schriften aus der Emigration ' (Vol. III, p. 344. German Edition).

After the surrender at Világos, Kossuth took refuge in Turkey, and in September, 1849, was interned at Widdin on the Danube, while every effort was being made by the Austrian and Russian

Envoys at Constantinople to secure the surrender by the Porte of the Hungarian refugees.

Strong pressure was put upon the Sultan by the Ambassadors of these two Powers to compel the unconditional ' extradition of all refugees, Poles and Hungarians, without entering into any distinction of political or criminal offences.' (Sir Stratford Canning to Viscount Palmerston, Therapia, August 25th, 1849. ' Correspondence respecting Refugees from Hungary within the Turkish Dominions.' Presented to Parliament, February 28th, 1851).

Count Julius Andrassy, the representative at Stamboul of the Hungarian Revolutionary Government, notified the fugitives at Widdin that the only way to save themselves would be for them to turn Mussulman.

There were at Widdin, at this critical moment, two foreign friends of Hungary—General Guyon, who had served in the Hungarian Revolutionary Army, and C. F. Henningsen—both warm partisans of the Hungarian cause. Kossuth, in his ' Memoirs ', records how, when this news arrived from Andrassy, it was Henningsen who advised him to write to Lord Palmerston begging him to come to the rescue of the refugees by throwing the weight of England into the balance in the sore-beset counsels of the brave Sultan—pressed and threatened by the representatives of the two great military despotisms of Eastern Europe. Kossuth goes on to say :

' I followed his advice and wrote the letter. But it was a ticklish question how to get the letter quickly to Palmerston's hands, because every minute was precious, and might have decided between life and death. We were poor; we had no courier to send to England. The post from Widdin was slow, and at the same time unreliable; letters had to pass through Austria, and we could be sure on the point that the " black Cabinet " at Vienna would take very good care that my letter should not reach Palmerston.

' I was surrounded by spies. I was quartered in the house of the Chief of the Police at Widdin. In the absence of any other resource, we decided to send my letter to the British Consul at Belgrade, and to request him to despatch it post-haste to England under his own official seal. But even that seemed to be a very long and wearisome way.

' While we were anxiously discussing this matter, a man hurried into my room—a typical-looking Englishman, with his hat pushed back, an umbrella under his arm, tired and dusty. We could see at once that he had come a long journey and just arrived.

' " Good day, gentlemen!" '

' " Good day, sir! What can I do for you?" '

' " I am come from India to fight for Hungarian freedom; but it seems to me I have come too late." '

' " Alas! too late, as you see. Please take a seat." '

. . . . .

' Henningsen whispered into my ear:

' " Never mind that letter " (to the British Consul at Belgrade). " We have got now a courier who will not stop till Downing Street." '

' " Who is it?" enquired I.'

' " This man," replied he.'

' " Do you know him?" '

' " No—but he is an Englishman; that is quite sufficient." '

' He approached the man and tapped him on the shoulder. " Sir." '

' " What is the matter?" '

' " Is your passport in order?" '

' " Yes." '

' " Have you money?" '

' " Yes." '

' " Very well—this is how the matter stands." (He explained the situation to him). " Life and death depend upon a single minute. We want a man who will go to London without a stop— who will not sleep or rest until this letter is placed into Palmerston's hands. Will you do that?"

' The brave Englishman jumped up from his chair, extended his hand towards me, and said nothing, but—

' " Where is the letter?" '

' I handed it to him, he stuck it into his knapsack, pulled his hat over his eyes, and saying—" All right—good-bye!" tore out of the room.'

' He did not mention his name, so that we could not know to whom we owed thanks.'

' A quarter of an hour had not elapsed when we heard the clatter of horses' hoofs in the street. It was he. Accompanied by a *cavass* he was galloping westwards. He made use of the quickest means of locomotion, and did not stop or take a rest until my letter was in the hands of Lord Palmerston.'

'The letter was published, too, and created a sensation; not on account of its form, but on account of its contents.

'When during my stay in America I was travelling to the Niagara Falls our train stopped at a station to let the train coming from the opposite direction pass. At the wish of the assembled multitude, I stepped to the carriage-window. From the window of the passing train a man's arm was stretched out and handed me a card. I took it. It bore the name—"Mr. Roger Casement," and underneath, in pencil, the words: "I handed to Palmerston the letter from Widdin."

'Thus I got to know the brave man's name. I have not heard another word from him since. May God's richest blessings follow him on his way, if he is still alive, or rest on his dust or his memory if he is dead.'

Kossuth's gratitude was not undeserved; but the brave 'Englishman' who at this critical moment of his career, hastening from India to fight for the freedom of Hungary, came to the rescue of the defeated and well-nigh abandoned leader in that, the darkest hour of Hungarian National life, was no Englishman—but an Irishman.

It was no instinct born of British Imperialism which had impelled this man to offer himself in the cause of Hungarian liberty. This friend of Hungarian freedom was one in heart and soul with the cause of Ireland. Born in the North of Ireland in 1819, Roger Casement came of a family settled for a considerable period in the County of Antrim. Roger Casement, although an officer in the British army, was, throughout his life, an ardent and sincere lover of Ireland—one who sacrificed something to his country, and never wavered in his loyalty to her National claims. It was to the sympathy inspired by the picture of Ireland in his heart, and to an overmastering love of freedom born of a close perception of the evils of Irish misrule that Kossuth owed the appearance at Widdin of his Irish deliverer.

The writer often, as a child, heard from Roger Casement's lips the story of his ride through Transylvania—when crushed Hungary was overrun with Austrian and Russian troops—with Kossuth's letter hidden in the heel of his boot. He literally never rested until his task was fulfilled. On one occasion he came near capture by a detachment of Austrian soldiers at an inn at which he had halted to change horses. On another occasion he was chased by a Russian patrol, but succeeded in outstripping his pursuers, and

Roger Casement during the Congo investigations.

British soldiers evicting farmers in Ireland.

Armed British police raiding a farmer's cottage in Ireland.

for the rest his passport carried him past too curious investigation.

The letter was personally given to Lord Palmerston at dinner, and the first unhurried meal its bearer took was that with the Foreign Minister himself as he recounted the story of the mission confided to him by Kossuth.

That letter served its purpose. Whether the chivalrous courage of the Sultan might have been overborne by the insistence of the Imperial bullies of Vienna and St. Petersburg, had not the weight of the British Foreign Office—never so respected as when directed by Lord Palmerston—been thrown into the scale on the side of the fugitives, it is hard to say. Probably not; but for that timely intervention, whatever its actual weight may have been, Kossuth was indebted not as he unwittingly supposed and states, to the ' English character ' with its ' wonderful energy and untiring perseverance,' but to a far other character and widely differing tradition—one, indeed, often derided and denied existence by that same English character—an Irishman's innate sympathy with the oppressed and enmity towards the oppressor. The man who came to help Kossuth at Widdin was an Irishman who would gladly have done for Ireland what he sought to do for Hungary.

Hungary has kept her proud place among the nations: Ireland has lost hers despite the traditional patriotism and diffuse ardour of her sons. Probably because of this very diffuseness. At home in all lands but their own—with ' too many strangers in the house ' —while they have ever been moved to give their lives in the cause of human freedom, Irishmen have too easily looked abroad for the realisation of those ideals which, had they looked more deeply within themselves, they would find can only flower on the soil which gave them birth.

The founder of modern Hungary saw clearly what we, as a race, have hitherto failed to see. In his ' Memories of My Exile' speaking of the struggle for Italian independence in 1859, Kossuth says:—

'However, in spite of all this, Italian unity became a reality. The Emperor Napoleon, so far from wishing for a united Italy, steadily opposed its realisation. Italy *was* nevertheless united. Not a single power in Europe wished for it, and still it became an accomplished fact.

' This carries with it a lesson for other nations. Let them survey the conditions of their national existence; and if this existence is rooted in history, which alone does create nations, while nature only produces nationalities—and there is a great difference between the two—time will bring the realisation, unless the nation spontaneously abdicates. Abdication alone means death to a nation.

' Is it that Ireland is indeed only a nationality, and not a nation? The answer must be given by Irishmen—and soon, for longer sleep must end in abdication.

' Italy was no nation before the coming of the House of Savoy—not even a nationality—(she was many nationalities)—yet she has evolved out of more conflicting elements than those which afflict Ireland today, a great national existence.

' The question ever before her was—How to become a nation, an independent and united nation? The desire to accomplish this was nourished for centuries, and national union was the result of it. A united Ireland will be an independent Ireland.'

'X'.

(i.e. Roger Casement.)

Chapter V

JOURNEY TO BRAZIL AND THE AMAZON

During this time Casement lived in Antrim and was one of the organisers of the first Feis to be held in the Glens of Antrim. He was the committee member for Glenshesk, and like every other project in which he engaged he worked whole-heartedly with his fellow-organisers often into the early hours of the morning. He inspired his friends and neighbours to take an interest in the history and customs of the Glens, and worked very hard to revive an enthusiasm for the old Irish folk dances and it gave him great delight to see as a result of his efforts the Irish jigs, reels, and horn-pipes being danced with vigour and enjoyment at the cross-roads.

At the same time he became closely associated with the leaders of the new movement for Irish independence which was eventually to displace the Redmondite party, viz., the Sinn Féin organisation. This body was the forerunner of the Irish Volunteers and in later times became the Irish Republican Army. He found that the ideals of these men and their love of Ireland, her language, and her culture, coincided with his own views and feelings. His preoccupation with Irish affairs led him to make a deep study of each and every method designed to make Ireland a free country and mistress of her own destiny. His own views are revealed in this letter:

' In God's name what Ireland wants is Responsibility. Until the public here feel that they *must* tackle the state of their own country and abide by their own acts there can be no real improvement. We have to create a governing mind again after 106 years of abstraction of all mind from this outraged land. We had once all the elements of a healthy national life in our midst—and because she feared us possessing those England destroyed our Constitution, juggled our mind out of our body into hers, and left us only a " corpse on the dissecting table." How are we to get back any healthy national consciousness through this conciliation scheme I fail to see, and I think Mr. Griffith is more than justified in his criticisms of the whole lot. . . .'

' The English beat the Irish solely because they had no music in their souls and were capable of any cold-blooded crime—and they are just the same race today . . . .'

' What a shameful system it is—an Irishman may do anything in the world for other countries but let him not dare to lift a finger for Ireland . . . .'

' The Anglo-Saxon remains always the Anglo-Saxon and is incapable of argument that does not set out from the standpoint that he must be in the right to begin with. . . . There is *so* much to do in Ireland it seems horrible to be going away from it—and God knows when I shall get back.'

The next year was spent in Santos, Brazil. He set out for there from Ireland in September, 1906, to take up the appointment of Consul for the States of San Paulo and Panama. He wrote aboard the ship:

' There is a huge and mighty sea roaring on the sand—a voice from far off deeps, and I must go out to look at the waves and

hear the sea before I go into that eminently English-minded Santos
where coffee (pelf) rules the day. . . . .

' I am not in the mood for writing—my surroundings too un-
congenial, although I am lucky in having a cabin all to myself. We
got to Santos on 9th October, Rio on 8th and the first Brazilian
port, Bahia, on 4th October. I am told Pernambuco is interesting
and is called the " Venice " of Brazil—but no one ever goes ashore
there, as they are afraid of sharks and being capsized into their jaws
—I think, after a West African surf boat and Congo canoe I shall
not quail before the Pernambuco sharks. All one's thoughts are
really with Ireland—if only one could see daylight . . . . '

' I have been reading Mitchel's Life to-day—it makes one moan
to think of the difference in the Ireland of his day and of ours.
To-day we have no ghost of a Mitchel—and the people are dead—
and only half Irish I often think.'

Then in December, 1907, he was transferred to Para and at the
end of 1908 he was made Consul-General at Rio de Janeiro, the
capital city of Brazil. He did not care much for Santos and he found
the social life there unattractive. The English colony he described as
' of the shop-keeping class of Englishman, without patriotism or
belief, or any charm or ideas at all '. Rio de Janeiro he liked better
and shortly after arriving there he heard the rumours which were
current about the scandalous treatment of the native population in
the region of the upper Amazon. The Company responsible for the
exploitation was the British registered Peruvian Amazon Rubber
Company, Ltd., with headquarters in London. The Company's
activities were carried on in the district of the upper Amazon known
as the Putumayo.

Casement went promptly to London and while there he had
many conferences with the Foreign Secretary, Sir Edward Grey. In
July he was asked by Sir Edward Grey to carry out an investigation
and enquiry into the state of affairs then prevailing in the Putumayo.
He was accompanied by five commissioners who were appointed by
the Peruvian Amazon Company.

Chapter VI

THE PUTUMAYO ATROCITIES

At Manaos, the capital of the State of Amazonas in Brazil, Casement arrived on 16th August, 1910, and reached Iquitos on the 31st. Here he spent two weeks and then proceeded on the steamboat 'Liberal' up the Amazon to Putumayo. During the fortnight which he stayed in Iquitos he made careful enquiries into the conditions there. Abundant evidence was forthcoming that exploitation of the natives was carried out on an immense scale and associated with shocking cruelties. The white agents were responsible for committing the most serious crimes which included flogging, torture and murder.

Needless to say every effort was made by the guilty persons to prevent their misdeeds coming to light. Witnesses were bribed, bullied, threatened, and on occasions ambushed and kidnapped. Casement was himself in constant peril from the forces behind the criminal system responsible for those atrocious crimes which through his agency were dragged to light. He wrote:

'Every chief of section was a law unto himself, and many of the principal agents of this British company were branded by the representative of that company, holding its power of attorney, in conversation with me, as "murderers, pirates, and bandits."'

From what he had heard, Casement was quite prepared to meet with shocking crimes, but the unspeakable horrors which he had to record were enough to make one physically sick. It was almost past the ingenuity of the most criminal mind to devise such barbarities as were inflicted on this docile and peaceful people by the white administrators of this British Company. Dealing with some natives of the Barbadoes who had been imported to work, in Casement's report one reads:

'The third incident I would cite is that of a native of Barbadoes named Joshua Dyall. He, like the two preceding men, was engaged in Barbadoes at the end of 1904, and was one of the party that went to Matanzas under Sanchez and Normand. This man, like most of the Barbadoes men, was passed from one station to another, and in the year 1907 he was serving at the station of Ultimo Retiro, where he was grossly maltreated by the agent, Alfredo Montt, who was then chief of the district, and who at the date of my visit was the company's representative in the district of Atenas. Montt charged Dyall with having improper relations with the concubine of one of the white employees, all of whom, it should be stated, kept Indian women, many of them more than one. The accused man was hung up by the neck, beaten with machetes, and then confined by the legs in heavy wooden stocks, called locally a " capo ". Each station is furnished with one of these places of detention. The stocks consist of two long and very heavy blocks of wood, hinged together at one end and opening at the other, with a padlock to close upon a staple. Leg-blocks so small as just to fit the ankle of an Indian are cut in the wood. The top beam is lifted on the hinge, the legs of the victim are inserted in two of these holes, and it is then closed down and pad-locked at the other end. Thus imprisoned by the ankles, which are often stretched several feet apart, the victim, lying upon his back, or possibly turned face downwards, remains sometimes for hours, sometimes for days, often for weeks, and sometimes for months in this painful confinement. Prisoners so detained are released from these stocks only to obey the call of nature, when for a few moments, guarded by armed men, they enjoy a brief release. Some of these implements of torture that I saw ready for use had nineteen leg-holes. In one case I counted twenty-one. The stocks at Ultimo Retiro, where Dyall was confined, were in my opinion, the cruellest of those I actually saw. The ankle holes were so small that even for an ordinarily well-built Indian, when closed the wood would often have eaten into the flesh. For an ordinary-sized European or negro the top beam could not close upon the leg without being forced down upon the ankle or shin-bone, and this was what happened to Dyall. He and the men who had witnessed his imprisonment assured me, that to make the top beam close down so that the pad-lock could be inserted in the staple two men had to sit upon it and force it down upon his legs. Although more than three years had passed since he suffered this punishment, both his ankles were deeply scarred where the wood (almost as hard as metal) had cut into the ankle flesh and sinews. The man's feet had been placed four holes apart—a distance, I should say, of from three to four feet—and with his legs thus extended, suffering acute pain, he had been left all night for a space of fully twelve hours. When released next day he was unable to stand upright, or to walk, and had to reach his quarters crawling on his belly propelled by his hands and arms. I saw the stocks just as they had been used to confine him. I caused a man of ordinary stature, a Barbadoes man, to have his legs enclosed before me. The stock did not close upon his legs, and to have locked the two beams together at the end could only have been done by great pressure and weight exerted upon the top beam, so as to force it down upon the leg and thereby undoubtedly inflict much pain, and cause lasting wounds.'

The native Indians were not only put in these stocks, but while in them were cruelly flogged and left sometimes for weeks. Sometimes after these floggings they were beheaded or shot. Men, women and even children were so tortured and killed. Casement estimated that up to 90 per cent. of the native Indians showed the scars of such savage floggings.

Another case brought to his notice was that of a native Indian woman who was brought into the station with a chain round her neck. She was taken outside and shot, her head cut off and displayed to the other natives present with the warning that they would get the same unless they carried out orders. The following is an extract from Casement's summary of the sworn evidence of Stanley Lewis:

' He often saw Indians flogged at Ultimo Retiro very often; they were badly cut, sometimes each time they got a lash the flesh would be cut. They were staked to the ground, and naked, and he has known them to die after flogging. The wounds would get maggots in them and then fester, and the house even became foul smelling from the number of these people in this condition. They would then be taken away and shot. He has seen men and women shot like this.'

The wretched native Indians when they found that the load of rubber which they had brought did not reach the required weight, automatically prepared for the expected flogging. In Casement's report an agent's evidence reads:

' The Indian is so humble that as soon as he sees that the needle of the scale does not mark the ten kilograms, he himself stretches out his hands and throws himself on the ground to receive the punishment. Then the chief or subordinate advances, bends down, takes the Indian by the hair, strikes him, raises his head, drops it face downwards on the ground and after the face is beaten and kicked and covered with blood the Indian is scourged.'

It is no wonder that Casement was horrified and nauseated by the savage brutality which these agents visited upon the defenceless natives, and that he resolved to draw the attention of the world to these iniquities.

An endless account of the most revolting cruelties and tortures, beheadings, burnings alive, beating and clubbing to death, is to be found in these reports.

One of the most notorious of these criminals was Normand, of whom Casement said:

' The crimes committed by this man are innumerable, and even Peruvian white men said to me that Normand had done things that none of the others had done.' One account of some of Normand's brutalities appeared in *Truth*. In this account he is reported to have burned alive a native chief before the eyes of his wife and children. He then beheaded the wife and dismembered the children and threw their bodies into a fire. Another testified that he had often seen Normand give as many as 200 lashes to the natives. This witness also saw him cut to pieces a native woman for not undertaking to live with one of his servants. Casement's report of the evidence of this witness continues:

' He saw Normand on one occasion take three native men and tie them together in a line, and then with his Mauser rifle shoot all of them with one bullet, the ball going right through. He would fire more than one bullet into them like this.'

But it is needless to give further instances of the horrors to which these unfortunate natives were subjected. Casement must have been heartbroken to have to record this revolting account of ' man's inhumanity to man '.

On November 16th he set out on his return trip down the Amazon to Para, and took the first ship back to London, carrying with him an extensive collection of documentary evidence exposing the wicked practices of the white administrators, and the inhuman sufferings of the native population.

In the beginning of 1911, a few weeks after his return, he supplied to Sir Edward Grey a summary of the evidence which he had collected. This he did with the object of getting criminal proceedings set on foot against one of the worst criminals whom Casement named in this précis. Towards the end of January, and again in March, he laid before Sir Edward Grey a full and detailed report of the administration of the Putumayo district, and the cruel oppression of the native inhabitants.

In June, 1911, Casement's name appeared in the Honours list, as an appreciation of his humanitarian work on behalf of the native population in the upper Amazon district of the Putumayo. This knighthood, conferred on him without any previous notice or suggestion, took him by surprise and he found it impossible to refuse acceptance of the unsolicited honour. A consideration which finally decided him in accepting was the fact that his work in the cause of the Putumayo Indians was yet unfinished, and refusal would mean resigning his position and leaving these unfortunate people still to suffer under tyranny and oppression. His letters make this clear:

'Very few can possibly believe that I have not worked for this— for a " distinction ", " an honour "—or whatever they call it— instead of, in reality, deeply desiring *not* to get it. I couldn't help it at all—and could not possibly fling back something offered like that. Yes it was Sir E. Grey—I had a charming letter from him telling me it was he did it. . . . I want you, please, to keep always writing to me just as " Roger Casement "—will you? That will be a distinction now. If Irish hearts that know my real feeling will keep on addressing my letters in the old way it will be a little consolation —for oh! you don't know how I hate the thing. I know and appreciate all the good feelings that has prompted it on Sir E. Grey's part —but I cannot be happy with this thing—and I shall expect and hope that all who really care for me will omit the words.'

Of the Coronation in that year he wrote:

'This Coronation *sham* and *humbug* shows that—the most abject sham, with no tittle of reality, or manliness or national faith in it —simply a huge commercial " try on " to get money with a puppet show and *procession* at £5-5-0 a seat and for that they sell their churches, their sick beds and sick beings in hospitals, their clubs and sanctified privacies and aristocratic mansions.'

Prolonged delays in the settlement of the affairs in Putumayo followed: months of heart-break for Casement who used all his powers of persuasion to overcome official inactivity and indifference. In repeated interviews with Sir Edward Grey, he stresses the need for action, and in the end he set sail again in August, 1911, for the Putumayo, and reached Iquitos in October. He was disgusted to find nothing but corruption in the Courts, whose duty it was to arrest and punish the criminals. Out of 237 warrants only nine arrests had been made, and through the influence of the company directors warrants and arrests were annulled, and so he reluctantly came to the conclusion that no real effort had been made to administer justice and to punish the criminals who were inhumanly exploiting the natives. He wrote:

' It was abundantly clear that the company, or those who locally controlled the Putumayo in its name, having recovered from the shock of exposure and fear that followed the visit of the commissioners and myself in 1910, had determined to retain forcible exploitation of the Indians as their right by conquest and their surest means of speedy gain.' Also in this report he wrote of the native as ' a being of extreme docility of mind, gentleness of temper, and strength of body, a hardy and excellent worker, needing only to be dealt with justly and fairly to prove the most valuable asset the country possesses. Instead of this he has been from the first enslaved, bent by extortion and varying methods of forced labour and toil, not for his own advantage or the advancement of his country but for the sole gain and personal profit of individuals who have ever placed their own desires above the common welfare.' Casement left, infuriated by the continuation of this system of terror and oppression, and by the appalling indifference of those charged with administering the affairs of the country.

Proceeding direct to New York, he called on the British ambassador, Mr. Bryce, to whom he unburdened his feeling of frustration and his detestation of the wicked system prevailing in the Putumayo. Bryce suggested that Casement should personally inform the President of the United States, Mr. Taft, and some members of the American Government of the position. Promptly Casement went on to Washington where during three days he had repeated conferences with state officials, and with President Taft himself. This move had the desired effect, and shortly after Casement's return to London early in 1912 the reports and correspondence were published as a Blue Book. When the world became aware of the devilish atrocities of the Putumayo, a storm of indignation was raised and a public demand made for a speedy ending of the system. The matter was dealt with in scathing terms in the press of every country, and as a result the dreadful system of terrorism and persecution was finally abolished.

Referring to the exploitation of native populations, he wrote; —

' It is atrocious—and I know, not from my heart alone but from my *head* that it is true. . . . . Between Leopoldism on the Congo, Diazism in Mexico, and what I know of the Amazon rubber trade there are more human beings held to-day in hopeless slavery, accompanied by the most inhuman cruelty, than at the height of the overseas slave trade. That is, I am convinced, a literal truth. Africa no longer exports slaves—her people are enslaved at home to European capitalists—and in South and Central America an *enormous* extension of the most disgraceful slavery has taken place in the last 25 years—induced by American and other capitalists and by the upward price of rubber. This abominable thing has got to be fought wherever it lifts its head—and I am firm that we shall do it. . . . . If we free the Congo slave we smite the Mexican slaver—international humanity is the only check to international financial greed.'

But all this was not accomplished without a very severe strain on Casement's health and constitution. The effects of the fearful and revolting experiences involved in his work and investigations as well as the prolonged service in what are perhaps the two most unhealthy regions in the world, forced him to retire on pension in broken health in August, 1913. He never fully regained his health and during the remaining three years of his life which he devoted entirely to his own country, he collapsed on several occasions under the intense strain of his patriotic work.

CHAPTER VII

LAS PALMAS—ST. HELENA—CAPETOWN—GERMANY

Early in 1912 as an invalid he spent some time in Las Palmas in the Canary Islands where after some time his health improved somewhat. From there he wrote:

' Here I am in these delightful islands, although just at present I am not in a beautiful one—La Palma. The island is beautiful, but the town horrible—and I go away today for Tenerife and Las Palmas in Grand Canary. I have quite travelled since I landed at the latter place just three weeks ago today. At first I was very much in the doctor's hands and a good deal in bed, for the pain of this malady did not lessen after I left London. However, since I got to Orotava on Tenerife I began to get better and feel now that I may get rid of this horrid complaint—for a time at any rate.

' The weather has been mostly wet and often cold for this latitude —and many times I wished myself back in old Ireland—especially when with Father Ward, the curate of Falcarragh in Donegal. Him I last saw up there in September last and then I met him in the same hotel in Las Palmas when I landed—and the other day he came to Orotava, just to see the Peak. The Peak is a glorious sight at present —fully half of it, 6,000 feet, covered in snow and shining in the sun like ice. I came over here to La Palma, 65 miles west of Orotava, two days ago in a small coasting steamer—but am leaving again today for Orotava which I like best of all.

' I have been reading your " Old Irish World " again this morning with fresh pleasure—although whatever pleasure I find in the telling of the Irish story is, always, more than swallowed up in the pain, resentment and regret I cannot swallow before I come to the end of the tale. I cannot believe that such long persisted in and wholly evil policy as that of England in Ireland cannot bring, ultimately, disaster to the wrong-doer. The seeds were planted deep and may take long in springing to life—but they were scattered with a profuse hand, and the work was so malignly deliberate that the harvest, I think, is sure even if late. There is another aspect of English criminality in Ireland, I think, unique among the conquering wrongdoers of Christian times at any rate. All the invaders and exterminators of the Middle Ages, who wrought more or less similar destruction on weaker peoples, are today sorry for their forefathers' acts. They proclaim them as crimes—often deplore them in their histories—and well-nigh universally, as individuals, express regret and pity for the conquered and often shame for the deeds of their own ancestors. Not so the English in Ireland. The Spaniards in Peru, for instance, even in the first heat of the conquest and enslavements of the Indians, produced many historians and writers who, even then, saw the wrong inflicted and deplored it. Today no Spanish Peruvian but, in speech, denounces the crimes of the conquest and uplifts the memory of the murdered Incas. He is proud to call himself by an Inca name—Husscar, or Atahualpa, and to identify himself, so far as he can, with the past of the country. Here, in the Canary Islands, the thing is more marked. The original inhabitants, the Guanches, made a brave resistance to the Spaniards throughout the whole of the fifteenth century. They were conquered in the end and the islands annexed to Spain—and no one of recognised or *pure* Guanche blood is said to survive—but there must be much of it mixed in the blood of the invaders. Although today the people are as Spanish as the Spaniards of Spain they one and all denounce the very acts that put them where they are, in possession of these beautiful islands. One never meets a " Canario " and mentions the word " Guanche " but he will declare that they were " a very noble people " and that their ill-treatment by the Spaniards was a " shameful " thing. It is much more than a tradition—it is an established factor in the consciousness of the islanders. Here in this little town of La Palma I find a cross erected to commemorate the Conquest of the Island (about 1445 or so, I think) and to record the valour of both combatants—the Spaniards who attacked and won and the " heroes of the Guanches " who " shed their blood for their native land." Now contrast this with the record of English civilisation in Ireland—and say then what *do* the English not deserve! Although they came to a Christian people, highly civilised and of great kindness of heart, numerous and artistic and full of love of music, poetry and history—they not only sought to and did destroy nearly all that they found, and enslaved the remnant of the people left from centuries of war of massacre and extermination, but they have never, from that day to this, as a people, expressed one word of regret or erected one single monument or memorial to those they destroyed. On the contrary, instead of admitting their crimes and deploring them, as the descendants of the Spaniards have freely done, and attesting the worth of those they attacked, they have persistently sought to destroy the character of the Irish race and have never in word or act repented their infamous past.

' Many Irish families in later days, Penal times, came to these islands. The chief street of this little city of Santa Cruz de la Palma is " O'Daly "! The hotel whence I write you looks out on this little " Calle O'Daly." In the capital of the whole group, Santa Cruz de Tenerife, there is a " Calle Murphy," a " Calle O'Donnell " and a " Calle Cologan " (intended for O'Callaghan). In Orotava the Marquis of Candia, one of the potentates of the island (Tenerife), is a Cullen—and some of the noblest families there are of Irish Catholic descent. So that even in these little islands of the Atlantic we find the seed of the scattering. So, too, in early times, Brendan the Navigator came here—they say—and it was the memory of Brendan's voyage led Columbus to the West. The story of Brendan has never been put in its right place in history. Had Brendan been an English bishop or saint how the world would long since have rung with his voyage! The New World would have become by Brendan's pre-emption a British world by discovery as well as by occupation.

'When the first expeditions were being fitted out in Europe to "explore" the Canaries—a noble named de la Cerda got a grant from Pope Clement VI of the "Fortunate Islands"—as the Canaries were termed by long tradition. This was in 1344. The "English ambassador" we are told, greatly incensed lodged a protest, declaring that the term "fortunate isles" belonged to Great Britain! There were no other happy islanders! Even in their ignorance we see John Bull at home five centuries ago, just as today, convinced that he alone has all that is good and right, and appropriating the adjectives of worth, just as he has laid hands on all the lands of value. What a determined people!—determined to stand well in men's opinion, even when robbing them. . . .

'I am due to go on to Rio again, to my great disgust, by end of March—but the doctors all prohibit it—especially the last one I have consulted in the islands. He says it will simply mean this disease becoming permanent and incapacitating me for the rest of my days —so I may be driven to get out of return to Rio at all costs—even by resigning and asking to be pensioned off. . . . Better every day now and the doctor says if I take care I shall entirely win—although he says to go to Rio would be fatal. So I shall not go to Rio again, I think—that the medical opinion is unanimous about.

'Balfour's remark to A.E. is what I have always said of the man— a Home Ruler himself by sheer force of intellect—but a coward and a traitor, too, in deed. So the Irish Party was once " one of the most ennobling "! Granted—it was a party of a great ideal and of un-compromising faith in its ideal. And how did Mr. Balfour *then* treat it? He put its leaders and members in jail—he termed them and treated them as criminals and used all the powers of his office and Government to destroy that " ennobling " party! And now it is " the basest." Granted, perhaps, again. And why? Because it has allied itself with and adopted the compromising methods of the English Party system. Because indeed it has become English. If that is to be base I agree with Mr. Balfour. If the Irish Party is base today it is because English Parties—Liberal and Conservative—are base and the Irish have joined with them *to secure by English methods* the thing they failed to secure by " ennobling " methods when Mr. Balfour admired them so much. What liars and shams these English are! And Mr. B. would give Ireland " a *far* better Bill "—what!— an Ireland that has no " national history "—no " national conscious- ness " and never was a nation or had a Parliament! What liars and shams!

' There are several things in life—and in human affairs on which no compromise is possible—nationality is one.

' I am sending lots of things out to the Dutch fighting in South Africa for their language, and I think I may go on there in a day or two perhaps to see my brother in the Orange Free State. The voyage will do me good—for there is less sun here than I need and the air and heat there, too, as well as on the voyage would be good for this complaint. I seriously think of going and if so shall sail in *Grantully Castle* from this on 6th instant.

' The Home Rule debate not so good—I missed the " ennobling " height—that point of view admitting of no compromise—a people's right, a nation's purpose. That note has never been struck and Redmond's pitiful references to " the Empire " justify Balfour's present contempt . . . . if the British people clearly and finally asserted their intention of re-establishing an Irish Parliament then Belfast and " Ulster " will, after splutters and protests, be forced into passive acceptance.

' Those are my views and have been now for over a year. The crux of the Home Rule problem is " Ulster ". Two factors are against Ulster—time and the tendency of the British people to regard Home Rule as inevitable and as a good thing imperially. These two factors will bring Home Rule—but I doubt much if Asquith *or* Redmond will be the instruments of its coming.

' I know Ulster men much better than John Simon—and I don't care a fig for the *Times* desertion of them. Until those men are convinced that they *can't* prevent Home Rule they will fight and now they are really convinced that they *can* prevent it—whether Asquith and Balfour were both against them.

' In the end they will abandon this idea—but they hold it now I think and what they believe they are very strong and sure to hold by. I think the Ulster men are the best part of Ireland in many ways

—and they should be convinced by appeals to their sense of justice, affection, and at bottom, love of Ireland. . . . We shall get to St. Helena tomorrow night—there may be time to go on shore and run up to Longwood to see Napoleon's living grave—but I doubt—as they are hurrying today and reach Capetown on 24th.

'We get to Capetown, D.V., on 24th, tomorrow week, and I shall very soon after go up country to my brother's place at Witzies Hoek in the Orange Free State where it is warm, dry and peaceful. . . . Please remember *any* light portable pamphlets on Irish language or Irish nationality will be of help to the Cape Dutch. I am going to give a copy of your "Nationality" to General Hertzog—and a few more *leaflets*—including the famous one of Stephen Clark fame! I've got some samples with me.

'I am now in my tenth day on board this very slow ship—and have practically been lying down the *whole* time—I've not walked quarter a mile since coming on board! I feel the pain at times, and am simply an invalid—there's no getting over that. . . . .

'I lunched yesterday with Major MacBride who led the Irish Brigade in the Boer War. He did splendid work there and I begged him to *write* that story—to leave on record the fight that little band of Irishmen (300 strong) made for Boer freedom. It was a fine fight and should be told, especially the capture of the guns at Colenso! It was the Irish Brigade got first then and it was MacBride who received the surrender of Colonel Bullock. I never knew that till yesterday. His story of the surrender of the Colonel is fine, especially when the Englishman found—at last—he had surrendered to an Irishman! You can imagine the feelings of an English Colonel who had given up his sword to an Irish "rebel"! Isn't it a picture. . . . .'

In May he visited Germany and was very favourably impressed with the German people and commented in letters home on their wonderful capacity for work, their intelligence, their industry, and their splendid methods of organisation.

AT THE GAELIC LEAGUE IRISH COLLEGE IN CLOGHANEELY,
CO. DONEGAL, 1904.

Front row :—Professor Seamus Searcaigh (U.C.D.) and Roger Casement.
2nd row:—Professor Eamon Ó Tuathail (T.C.D.) and Professor Agnes O'Farrelly.
3rd row :—Mr. Padraig Carr and Rev. Brother Malachi.

Gun running by the Orangemen at Larne, Co. Antrim, 2nd May, 1914.

CHAPTER VIII

REBELLION IN ULSTER

Retired, living in Ireland on his pension, and in broken health, one would imagine that Casement's life work was done. He wrote:—

'I am, as usual, wading through troubled waters here, but things shape better daily and my "grave indiscretion" in likening Connemara to the Putumayo has after all done *only good*. That is clear. No one I find reproaches me and all were secretly glad—some openly so and at any rate widespread public attention has been called to the evil and wicked plight of the poor people—a remnant of Cromwellian civilisation sitting in the *Embers* of the hell or Connacht then decreed the doomed Irish race. I go there very soon.

'I *must* leave Ireland again and go back to South Africa I think. Great trouble is there on my poor brother and his wife and I feel I must go to him. I should never forgive myself if I did not try to save that sinking house.'

But his master passion, the liberation of his country, would not permit him to rest. First of all he became interested in Irish education, and as a result became associated with P. H. Pearse in the establishment of St. Enda's School at Rathfarnham, an institution in which the pupils were given a knowledge of the history of their country and instruction in the Irish language.

A request from the headmaster of his old school, the Ballymena Academy, brought a reply from Casement which is illuminating. The following is an extract:

'I fear I could not give very much help, for I have already promised over £100 this year to educational efforts in Ireland that are directed to a national end. . . . . These are a training college in Donegal, an Irish school in Galway and a school in Dublin (St. Enda's) where the course of teaching is Irish throughout, that is, a course devised primarily to interest boys in their own country and make them good and useful citizens of it. . . . . I was taught nothing about Ireland in Ballymena School—I don't think the word was ever mentioned in a single class of the school—and all I know

33

of my country I learned outside the school. . . . . . Patriotism has
been stigmatised and often treated as " treason ", as a " crime ", or
dismissed with superior scorn as: " local ". . . . . As an Irishman,
I wish to see this state of things changed and Irish education to be
primarily what that of every healthy people is—designed to build up
a country from within, by training its youth to know, love and
respect their own land before all other lands.'

Living in County Antrim, not far from Belfast, he found himself
in the centre of the commotion consequent on Carson's organising
the Orangemen there against Home Rule for Ireland. He was
mortified to see his hopes of a free and united Ireland smashed by
the action of Messrs. Carson and F. E. Smith and their followers in
co-operation with one of the two large political parties in England.
The Orangemen were drilled and armed to resist an impending act
of the British Parliament which would afford a measure of autonomy
to Ireland. This defiance of parliament, in addition to Carson's
public statement that he would break any law to gain his ends,
convinced Casement that the parades and military exercises of the
Orangemen must be countered by an organisation composed of
those who believed in Irish freedom. As an Irish patriot whose life's
ambition was to see his country free, he was naturally angered to see
these lawless armed bands of Orangemen defying the popular will of
the country, as well as the expressed will of the British parliament.

His letters show his activities at this time:—

' With the help of every drop of Fenian blood in my soul I hope
will light a fire there may set the Antrim hills ablaze. . . . It is
that sorry " sympathy " for Ireland I mean to bury on the Antrim
platform—and to unite (for I think it is possible) Presbyterian and
Catholic farmers and townsmen at Ballymoney in a clear message
to Ireland. . . . It will mark the beginning of the uprising of the
North.

' It will be a meeting, mind you of *extraordinary* significance
from the heart of Antrim, by Antrim men, Presbyterians and Protestants and a flaming appeal to Ireland. It will breathe much of
the spirit of '98 and will be definitely Irish—not of an English
party at all. I go on to the Glens end of week—please God, to
arrange about the meeting at Ballymoney. . . . .

' The Review was good as a spectacle—but Carson's face was
awful. He looked " the Chief traytour of Ireland—a reprobate

reserved for the sword ". I think the man is very unhappy—he looked wretched, gloomy, dark and foreboding, and the shadow of the Castle and its " bloodhounds " was over him, and the greater gloom even of the bloodshed yet to be. I am not against bloodshed in a good cause—but for this.

' I got ill and had to go straight to bed in a Coleraine Hotel with a bad fit of shivers and agues, and was kept there by the doctor till yesterday.

' I feel I *could* not do anything else but go out and join the " grim, hard, determined Ulster face " when I see it being shot at by Tommy Atkins. In fact, I'm absolutely certain I'd go! But I like Stacpoole's line of thought about Ireland and her spirit making one her children all. That's the right thought. . . . .

' It is that aspect of life is so appalling in Ireland. In the South and West where one finds spiritual and intellectual kinship with the gentler Irish mind, one is forced to confess, too, it is blurred by the long contact with the depression of the penal swamp in which the people were plunged for so long and out of which they are only climbing slowly. One is conscious that one is talking to men who are not yet quite free and still have the fears and weaknesses of slavery round them. And up here where they are free, with a great freedom, it is the freedom of the wild beast. They have no spiritual, no intellectual freedom of their own—and they will not allow others to have it. It is coming—painfully coming—but until it comes Ireland is a hard country to live in. . . . .

' I have *always* said, as you know, that the Government would be beaten on Home Rule, and that even if they made the Bill an Act it would still never produce an Irish Parliament in being. I have not wavered in that opinion—only for a brief day or two when Carson was at the height of his blasphemies over here—I thought " perhaps *this* will open the eyes of all that is best in John Bull and stiffen his resolution "—but it was only for a shade of a thought. I knew it wouldn't—and everything goes to show that the leopard cannot change his spots. The British public is actually in love with " Rebellion in Ulster "! My God—how they utterly sicken me, this English people. When one thinks of John Mitchel and the Famine and all that starving, persecuted, outraged Ireland then had to fight against, and how England met *that* fight for human existence!—and now, when these infuriated and selfish bigots, who have suffered no wrong, no threat, no injury to a hair of their heads go out in thousands to break the law, to arm and drill against Crown and Parliament, they are taken to the bosom of that great Constitutionalist. The whole thing is so utterly atrocious—I feel I have no heart to try and plead. I feel far more disposed to go to Athlone, to Dublin, to Galway and plead there and say: Rise—men of Ireland—and arm, too. Arm yourselves to defend your land, your homes and assert your freedom as men —that is the task that Ulster sets you. Follow her lead, and in the day of trial Ireland shall win her freedom by her own strong heart and arm. . . . . .

'If I tell Englishmen the truth and what I think of them in Ireland I may shut up shop—they'll never listen again—and if I tell Irishmen their salvation cometh from the Liberals, I tell them what I don't believe—and what I do believe to be a lie. Civil war would be *far* better than to go on lying and pretending—if only we could be left free to fight out our battle here ourselves. I am so sick of the English.

'Individually I like many—collectively I loathe them. As men they are often very good men, very fine men—as an institution they are repellent to my whole nature—and as an institution they have been a curse in Ireland transcending all the maledictions of history. And they are at it still—God save Ireland.

'I'd like to see some spirit arising in Ireland—something of this volunteer spirit of self-reliance—would it not, perhaps, be a better thing to try and stimulate that than to attempt " concili- ation " meetings up here where no conciliation is? If it be right and fine as the English say, for Ulster to arm and drill against those who have never hurt her—how much finer a thing it is for Ireland to arm and drill against those who have always hurt her. I think I'll end by going to Athlone, or Tipperary and seeing what can be done in that line. The alternative is so sickening to think of. Here it is. The Bill will *surely* be defeated—of that I am convinced. It will not affect the end at all, even if they pass it next June under the Parliament Act—it will still be defeated in the end—and the Tories will come in and either repeal it or suspend it—the same thing in fact. What will Ireland do? She will be asked by Redmond, Dillon and Co. to go on " trusting the Liberals "—to go on spouting I.P. isms on the U.I.L. platforms in Great Britain—to go on on the old, weary, soul destroying, national-life destroying English political party campaign—and all the time she will have been degraded lower than ever before.

'Emigration will go up—it *is* rising even now—and no healthy

thing will be *done* in all the land. The only healthy thing now is
this Volunteer movement up here. It is fine: it is the act of men;
and I like it, and love to think of those English Liberal Ministers
squirming before these Ulster men who say: " To Hell with
your politics—we mean to fight." If only Ireland arose and said:
" I, too, mean to fight!"—Then we might see daylight.

' Everyone (here in the Glens) thinks " Civil War " is in sight
and the ladies are, some of them, terrified. Civil war, of course,
means shooting Papishes. In my heart I think it is the only way
these outrageous people can ever be brought to their senses. If
only the British Providence would withdraw from the island for
six months and leave Ireland and " Ulster " to settle this question
man to man, we should at last see daylight in Ireland. But that
can never be—and so we shall have the British Providence in the
intervals of dining, insisting on looking in on Ireland and doing
the wrong thing at the usual intervals. I agree with all you say
about the public opinion being allowed to grow up in England and
Scotland—and yet *what* can one say that has not already been
said? No amount of " notes " will make an English or Scots
M.P. into an enlightened Irishman—or give him the local certainty of knowledge necessary to kick the liars and the " Ulster "
paid advocates out of the window of his hall. If only we could have
run a series of meetings up here as I hoped—or if Horace Plunkett
would but come out of his co-operative creamery and give us
something else than skim milk to drink—I am sick of that Co-
operative **Movement**.

' The population of Rathlin, by the way, was taken by our
teacher, Mr. Green. He found it (above 2 years of age) to be 325
persons. Of these 218 were Irish speaking and 107 spoke English
only, having no Irish at all, but of these 107 English speakers, 35
belonged to the lighthouses, public works, etc.—all imported people
for special work—so that of the island population itself—native born
—only 72 had no Irish. Of the 218 who spoke Irish only 10 were
non-native born—Irish from other parts of Ireland. So there is a
good big residuum of Irish speaking still in Rathlin to keep alive.

' Paddy Gallagher's views on Irish are far worse than that letter
indicated—the whole thing is pounds, shillings and pence—and
I have not met one " Economist " in the movement who had
saved his soul alive. All had ceased to have an ideal above poultry,
and if they had a country would only value it for what it would
fetch in the English market.

' Dillon, Redmond and Co.—bah!—they are as Irish as T. P. O'Connor. You see what is reported of their Irish dinner to the Premier—no Irish word of song or story at it. They are quite contemptible. . . . . As to the " arguments " of the lordly opponents of Home Rule—I do not see how one *can* argue with such exponents. . . . The one thing these people desire is that there should be no more Ireland. What they want is a dead land—and between them all it is what they will get.'

CHAPTER IX

ORANGEMEN ON THE WARPATH

On the 24th October a meeting was held in the Town Hall of Ballymoney, to protest against the lawless action of the Orangemen. At this meeting a resolution was passed expressing their refusal to agree to the exclusion of Ulster from the rest of Ireland. The *Times* commented in a sarcastic vein on this meeting with particular reference to some remarks made by Casement, who lost no time in replying:

' Your correspondent,' he wrote, ' is good enough to refer to me as one who " combines citizenship of the world with an enthusiastic attachment to romantic Nationalism ". . . . . It was doubtless an enthusiastic attachment to romantic humanitarianism that led my footsteps up the Congo and Amazon Rivers, and probably without that quality I should have failed in the very practical investigations I was privileged to conduct in both regions, and to bring to a not unsuccessful issue.

' That humanity has lost, from my being an Ulster crank or faddist of this kind, I must leave to a wider public to decide.

' I may say, however, that whatever of good I have been the means of doing in other countries was due in the first place to the guiding light I carried from my own country, Ireland, and to the very intimate knowledge I possessed not only of her present day conditions, but of the historic causes that led up to them.

' With a mind thus illumined, I was not ill-equipped for comprehending that human suffering elsewhere, however dissimilar that apparent environment might be, originated in conceptions of human exploitation that are both very old and very widespread and have not always been confined by civilised men to the merely savage or barbarous citizens of the world.

' Since a personal reference has been made to me you may pardon my adaptation of it, and admit that a wide outlook on human affairs is not incompatible with a very near insight into, and a close comprehension of, other things. For, unlike Sir Edward Carson, Lieutenant-General Richardson, Lord Charles Beresford, Mr. F. E. Smith and many of those who represent Ulster either in Parliament or on the " Provisional Government ", I am both by family and education an Ulsterman. My father and grandfather were both citizens of Belfast, and my family, for generations, has been closely associated with County Antrim life. I was educated at Ballymena in the centre of this county, and I know the people of Antrim from my early boyhood.

' The only " romance " of my nationalism is that it is wholly impersonal, and it is not associated with any party, or expectant of any party or personal gain. In this I believe I represent far more truly many, and a growing number, of the sturdy people of this kindly part of Ireland than those who misrepresent them as being aliens in their own land.

' It is true that I have not harangued or addressed Ulster audiences, but I have lived amongst Ulster people many years of my life, and in quiet and daily contact with them I have learnt to know them well. Many who read my remarks on Friday last have already assured me I spoke for them, and I doubt not that the note of love for Ireland then sounded by a small band of Ulster folk will yet be echoed on a score of platforms in this most Irish province of Ireland.'

About this time there appeared in the ' Fortnightly Review ' an article by Conan Doyle advocating the co-operation of Ireland with England in the event of a European war, and saying that Irish interests were identical with those of England, and added : ' If they imagine that they can stand politically or economically while Britain falls, they are woefully mistaken.' This was the same writer who had written and published in 1902 a propaganda book eulogising and justifying the action of England in attacking the Boer Republic and he now appeared once more in support of British Imperialism.

Casement answered Conan Doyle's article in a contribution to the ' Irish Review ', in the course of which he wrote :

' The conclusion that Ireland must suffer all the disasters and eventual losses defeat would entail on Great Britain is based on what may be termed the fundamental maxim that has governed British dealings with Ireland throughout at least three centuries. That maxim may be given in the phrase, " Separation is unthinkable ". Englishmen have come invincibly to believe that no matter what they may do or what may betide them, Ireland must inseparably be theirs, linked to them as surely as Wales or Scotland, and forming an eternal and integral part of a whole whose fate is indissolubly in their hands. While Great Britain, they admit, might well live apart (and happily) from an Ireland safely " sunk under the sea ", they have never conceived of an Ireland, still afloat, that could possibly exist, or be permitted to exist, apart from Great Britain. Sometimes, as a sort of bogey, they hold out to Ireland the fate that would be hers if, England defeated, somebody else should " take " her. For it is a necessary corollary to the fundamental maxim already stated that Ireland, if not owned by England, must necessarily be " owned " by someone else than her own inhabitants. . . . .

' That Ireland is primarily a European island, inhabited by a European people who are not English, and who have for centuries appealed to Europe and the world to aid them in ceasing to be politically controlled by England, is historic fact. . . . .

' I need not further labour the question. If Englishmen will but awaken from the dream that Ireland " belongs " to them and not to the Irish people, and that that great and fertile island, inhabited by a brave, a chivalrous and an intellectual race (qualities they have, alas! done their utmost to expel from the island), is a piece of real estate they own and can dispose of as they will, they cannot fail to perceive that the " Irish Question " cannot much longer be mis- handled with impunity, and that far from being, as they now think it, merely a party question—not even a " domestic question " or one the Colonies have a voice in—it may in a brief epoch become a European question.

' With the approaching disappearance of the Near Eastern ques- tion (which England is hastening to the detriment of Turkey) a more and more pent-in Central Europe may discover that there is a Near Western question, and that Ireland—a free Ireland—restored to Europe is the key to unlock the western ocean and open the seaways of the world.'

Chapter X

THE MENACE OF ARMED VIOLENCE

In the year 1913 Casement, who had always been a keen student of world affairs and who had the advantage of twenty years experience in the consular service, was convinced that war between England and Germany was inevitable, although he did not expect the outbreak until the year 1915.

It now became crystal clear to Casement that no time was to be lost in recruiting, drilling and arming the people of Ireland in defence of their rights. Some preliminary work had already been done in the way of organising in Dublin and some parts of the country by a group which was led by Professor Eoin MacNeill and Bulmer Hobson.

An energetic organising committee was now formed which included Casement, and one of the first acts was to publish ' A Manifesto of the Irish Volunteers ' which was prepared by Roger Casement and Professor MacNeill. It read as follows:

' At a time when legislative proposals universally confessed to be of vital concern for the future of Ireland have been put forward, and are awaiting decision, a plan has been deliberately adopted by one of the great English political parties, advocated by the leaders of that party and by its numerous organs in the Press, and brought systematically to bear on English public opinion, to make the display of military force and the menace of armed violence the determining factor in the future relations between this country and Great Britain.

' The party which has thus substituted open force for the semblance of civil government is seeking by this means not merely to decide an immediate political issue of grave concern to this Nation, but also to obtain for itself the future control of all our national affairs. It is plain to every man that the people of Ireland, if they acquiesce in this new policy by their inaction, will consent to the surrender, not only of their rights as a nation, but of their civil rights as men. . . . . If we fail to take such measures as will effectively defeat this policy, we become politically the most degraded

41

population in Europe, and no longer worthy of the name of Nation. . . . . In a crisis of this kind, the duty of safeguarding our own rights is our first and foremost duty. . . . . From time immemorial, it has been held by every race of mankind to be the right and duty of a freeman to defend his freedom with all his resources and with his life itself. The exercise of that right distinguishes the freeman from the serf, the discharge of that duty distinguishes him from the coward.

' To drill, to learn the use of arms, to acquire the habit of concerted and disciplined action, to form a citizen army from a population now at the mercy of almost any organised aggression—this, beyond all doubt, is a programme that appeals to all Ireland, but especially to young Ireland. . . . .

' The object proposed for the Irish Volunteers is to secure and maintain the rights and liberties common to all the people of Ireland. Their duties will be defensive and protective, and they will not contemplate either aggression or domination. Their ranks are open to all able-bodied Irishmen without distinction of creed, politics or social grade. . . . . . '

On the 25th November a historic meeting was held in the Rotunda which resulted in the founding of the Irish Volunteers. The enthusiasm of the crowd was tremendous, and thousands enrolled that same evening in the new force. Companies and battalions were formed without delay, drill instructors were appointed, officers elected, and in a short time the organisation spread throughout the whole country. Local committees for each town and county undertook the work of recruitment and training. Casement saw clearly that the immediate and urgent need was the provision of arms for the men who had enrolled. The Orangemen were by this time fully armed, and were still importing large consignments of rifles and ammunition, and a decree by the British Government at this juncture, totally prohibiting the importation of arms into Ireland, had the effect of leaving the Irish Volunteers completely unarmed. The unfairness of this discrimination aroused Casement's anger, and he wrote:

' Since the attitude of the Government is, to make arming illegal for Irishmen favourable to the policy of Irish national autonomy, while those opposed to it are allowed to arm and are assisted by the wealth of the governing classes of Great Britain.'

In Cork at an evening's meeting he enrolled seven hundred men as volunteers, and from this onwards under his inspiring direction the movement spread rapidly. Wherever he went the men came forward to serve, and the sense of solidarity and comradeship formed among these local units awoke in them an even stronger sense of nationality and inspired in them confidence and determination.

Casement's speeches were short and pointed, and could be summed up in his oft repeated injunction: ' Drill and arm.' Wherever he went he gave the same instruction. As a result drilling was now nation wide, but the tragedy was that no arms were available, and from this forward the prime aim and object of all his efforts was to endeavour to provide the necessary arms for the men. This search for arms was to lead him to America and to Germany where after nearly two years of ceaseless effort he succeeded in obtaining 20,000 rifles and 1,000,000 rounds of ammunition. But this is a story that must be told in some detail.

Visiting London in February, 1914, Casement made a thorough study of the European situation. As a result of shrewd enquiries and with his long diplomatic experience, he soon came to the conclusion that war between England and Germany was imminent. This discovery provided him with an added problem. In addition to finding arms for the Irish Volunteers he was now facing the task of trying to keep Ireland out of the impending war which he clearly saw was in reality just a contest between powerful trade rivals. With sound discernment he was convinced that England had no intention whatever of giving self-government to Ireland, and that she had already made a secret deal with Carson and the Orangemen. On his return from London in February, 1914, he gave expression to these views in a letter written to a friend:

' The game now, I see, is this. Under cover of " an offer to Ulster " they are going to strip all the flesh off the Home Rule Bill— if we let them. Shall we? That is for you and others to think over. Meantime I am convinced the right and patriotic thing for all Irishmen to do is to go on with the Volunteers: volunteers in every county, city, town, and village in Ireland. Don't despair of arms. I think we can get them. The Irish in America will not desert us in this crisis. I believe I can get you help from them the English little dream of today. . . . . The English are going to surrender to Carson.

' Don't despair—don't despond. We shall win, rest assured of that. Ireland was not born to suffering through the ages to end in death and despair at last. Her people have not kept their religion and their souls for nothing. . . . .

' This is the psychology of the situation. She (England) recoils from the Ulstermen, because they are *not* slaves—and she knows it. They tell her to go to hell, and propose to send her there, and you see, she draws back, talks of compromise " concession " while you and I, the mere Irish, are to take it in the old abject submission. Well, I for one won't—I mean to fight—and if John Bull betrays Ireland again, as I'm quite sure he means to do, then, with the help of God, and *some* Irishmen he'll learn that all Irishmen are not slaves and there is fight in us still.

' I'll get the arms yet—don't fear, fifty thousand of them—if you'll get the men ready.'

About this time the affair known as the ' Curragh Mutiny ' took place. Out of a total of seventy officers stationed at the Curragh command fifty-nine stated they would ' prefer to be dismissed ' rather than take orders from the Army Council to ' take active operations against the organised bodies of the Ulster Volunteer Force under their responsible leaders.' Brigadier General Gough was the ring-leader, but after some palaver the matter was smoothed over, and an undertaking was given by the English Government that these regiments would not be used to enforce the law.

It required little analysis of the situation to realise then that the Orange party were assured of the solid support of the all-powerful Unionist party in England, and that the Army was also on the side of the Orangemen. The solitary hope that remained for Irishmen to assert their right to freedom now lay in the Irish Volunteers, and more and more men came forward to serve in this force. Casement flung himself with ardour into this campaign. He wrote:

' I have in my mind a great scheme of Volunteers for all Ireland. To begin at Athlone. They have begun there already. I think we should strike while the iron is hot and get the thing on its legs for *all* time. " Ulster " has played into our hands! . . . .

' I go to Limerick tomorrow night—to be there on Sunday for a great Volunteer meeting—the Mayor to preside and I to be " Chief Speaker ". . . .

' The meeting last night was splendid—a great success in every way. Practical, earnest, well arranged and splendidly filled. The faces were handsome, strong and *good*—fine young men, and strong men and old men, too. Wealthy and poor—town and country were there—and no women admitted! All men. The Mayor presided. Mr. Pearse spoke splendidly—an orator. I was asked to be " the chief Speaker "—but I handed it over to him, for he was far fitter to make an oration than I—and it was that was wanted. I came second—without notes, or written word—just trusting to luck and the good sense of the meeting and I think I, too, was effective. I praised the North—and they cheered loudly—and I made jokes and was quite humorous and *talked*—not speechified. I told them two or three " stories " of Belfast—and I opened on the Boers and the Boer War for freedom and how that handful of brave men relying only on " Volunteers " in the cause of " freedom " fought the greatest Empire in the world for three years—and *now* were masters in their own house. They understood it all and cheered me to the echo.

' I ended quite unexpectedly. Mr. Pearse had said " the Irish were the only *white* race that was denied the use of arms ". I capped that. I said that I had lived most of my life with blacks and savages and *they* all were armed to defend their homes and all were Volunteers. There was *only one black race*—a race the English called "niggers" who were like the Irish, unarmed—" The only unarmed races in the world today," I ended quite simply, " are the Indians and the Irish!"—and I sat down. They cheered me for three minutes. . . .

' I believe Carson is in earnest—I think the Ulster men are and they have made him in earnest, I think they are the only honest part of the whole anti-Home Rule fight, and I believe they will go far further than Bonar Law. He is a cur—like A. J. Balfour and the rest.

' I have recently had put into my hands the most *extraordinary* evidence of the infamy of Balfour, Salisbury and Co. at the time of the *Times* attack on Parnell. It is a statement that, if published, would do more to wreck the *Anglo Saxon* Alliance than anything I have seen—if properly edited and written up. The evidence is there—the corruption is there; the shamelessness is there, the debauchery of the " public service " by the highest Servant of the State is there : all for political ends against Ireland. It is an epitome of English dealing with Ireland and might walk straight out of the Calendar of State papers of Tudor days. I will bring it to London if I get permission of its owner.

' At Limerick, strange to say, old John Daly the Fenian told me

(without any inkling of the document) just as a prison reminiscence
how Soames the lawyer of the *Times* came to him in jail and
threatened him if he would not denounce Parnell and implicate him
with the Phoenix Park killing (I won't call it murder—it was the
same *idea* impelled those poor, ignorant, *unselfish* Irishmen as
impelled Charlotte Corday, or Harmodius and Aristogriton).

'They tried first to bribe him to inform—and then when he
laughed them to scorn, Soames said, "We'll *drag* it out of you!"
"We'll compel you to tell!" What a government!—What a
country!—What a people to be in the grip of! Give me the Russians
rather—any open violence. . . . .

'Anyhow I'm going on for all I'm worth with the Volunteers.
They are the hope of the new Ireland—still the old, old Ireland,
always here.'

CHAPTER XI

POLITICAL INTRIGUE

' " Ulster " is out for one thing and one thing only, to defeat
and prevent Home Rule. You think she will accept a compromise
that ensures it. I don't. They will regard every offer from one
standpoint only—how far it is useful to prevent the Bill becoming
law—not how far it can be used to work the Bill to their advantage. They would much sooner have a row than a compromise
that conceded anything to their " implacable foes."

' Therefore, I have not the slightest anticipation that anything
serious will come of H.P.'s* mission. But your letter raised other
questions.

' First. You say you think the Cabinet are not greatly taken with
H.P., yet they send him to Ulster the bearer of their " offer ".
Are they acting very highly in this? Surely the " offer " on which
they mean to lay such stress in public should be entrusted to one
who was entirely trusted and one of themselves. That is a side
point—but it illustrates their methods of diplomacy.

' Second. As to South Africa—nothing we (Volunteers),
" Ulster ", H.P. or anyone or anything else can or cannot do will

---

* H.P. is Sir Horace Plunkett.

in the slightest affect the decision on that point. Like everything else that the British Parliament touches it will become a furious party question and will be debated *solely* on that account. The more they debate it the worse *nationally* for themselves.

'The Boers are masters of South Africa and nothing the so-called Imperial Parliament can say or do will alter one tittle of South African national policy. The people there will judge and decide their own issues—and all the British Parliament will gain, nationally, will be a further straining of the Imperial " tie " and a further growth of national feeling in South Africa. The only thing they could do of any effect is the thing they cannot do— go out and conquer South Africa again and depose the national Government. Therefore, their discussion will be futile in the extreme, for the professed end—but probably very disquieting for the unavowed but true aim—to embarrass the Government. Nothing we can do can prevent the " loyalists " of England from humiliating their country if they wish to do so—and that is one of their chief claims to existence.

'Third. As to the Volunteers I remain firm as a rock. Were we to shift or change with every change of party tactics in England we should be unworthy to begin the thing at all.

'The worth and high value of volunteering stares us in the face from Ulster. The *one* and *only* thing that stands in the way of the Home Rule Bill is that a handful of Irishmen have become Volunteers. The British Government (and " Constitution ") respect only one thing. The day we are as strong as Ulster there will be no whittling down of Home Rule. Redmond's mistake for 20 years has been to trust the Liberals. They will assuredly betray him in the end. Of that I have an entire conviction. The Bill is now such an attenuated and wretched thing—an abortion from the day it was born—that I doubt the possibility of it doing any good. Even the principle of Home Rule, however cribbed and cabined, I'd accept at a high price—but we do *not* get the principle of Home Rule here at all. The Imperial Parliament with its members from Ireland will be just as it is now—supreme and constantly on the spot. The *Government* of Ireland—the important thing of all—will still be at Westminster. What we want is a Government of Ireland in Ireland by Ireland, and that we are not going to get under this Bill or any means towards it that I can see. I would give them the " Parliament " with pleasure for an Irish Government.

'Fourth. As to my seeing Redmond. Redmond would no more

discuss Home Rule with me than, say, with Jack White. He probably looks upon us both in the same light. Redmond will not open his mouth to a soul outside the charmed circle of Dillon, Devlin and Co. and the party machine. He would not even see me. Besides, nothing would, in the least, be altered if he did see me.

' H.P., " Ulster ", South Africa, Bonar Law, the Labour revolt, etc., etc., all these things remain and will come to issue clear enough. Redmond can do nothing but sit tight—and *in private* say: " Well, if you whittle down the Bill *too* much, Ireland will reject it " (she will!) " and then you'll have to deal with a bigger Ulster."

' That is the political argument for the Volunteers as apart from the national—and it is a very sound one.

' I shall imitate Mr. Redmond and sit tight and go on quite quietly and firmly with the Volunteer movement. It will go on without me in any case—and I am not going to try and panic the others because English politics are upset—they always are. London is the centre of the greatest amount of political intrigue in all the world—just think of the strings pulled from there, under every sun people dance to them and under every sky die. The Boers will not. And if we can get the Irish Volunteers into a reality then, please God, Ireland will not. We've got to bring back manhood of mind no less than of body to Irishmen—and that is not to be made dependent on the intrigues of politicians. I am not the least bit alarmed. I have never, for a moment, believed this Bill will go through, and have always told you so.

' The Ulster resistance to Home Rule and victory by force over the mighty Liberal Government Party will be laid close to the heart of Ireland. We shall do the same thing on a bigger scale and gain a much bigger victory—and I think a final one.

' In any case, I feel the issue will be decided by brave men, by determined men, by sincere men—and not by wobblers. Ulstermen are all that, and in the first instance they are going to win *because* they are that and the opponents of Ulster are not. When we've got the same backbone and manhood asserted through the larger Ireland we shall see larger results.

' I am no good at tricks or " conversations " and I mean to keep quite clear of them. Let the politicians rage furiously together— the young men of Ireland will try to make themselves into men. That's my gospel of Irish salvation—it has been for years—and

ROGER CASEMENT.

Dublin after artillery bombardment during Easter week insurrection, 1916. Prisoners and civilians being marched to internment camps.

now the year has come, through the very follies of the politicians, that gives us the start.

'Worry won't alter facts—and the facts are that a section of Ireland means business and will win because it does. We have to apply that lesson to our souls and hearts and see that all Ireland shall mean business and get its work done as efficiently and well as the Ulster men are doing their smaller work.

'You see, my views are wholly non-" political "—I cannot think or act in a political or party sense. It is a constitutional failing, no doubt—but the insincerity, the make-believe, the *pose* of politics and above all of Westminster politics (that whited sepulchre staring the Abbey in the face!) entirely disgust me. I loathe them—and I am quite unfit to advise or act with politicians. I am, in every fibre, the " inordinate, wild Irishman ", and I *can* be nothing else. So it's no use at all asking me to enter into politics. . . . .

'Our dear Friend across the water (I mean the Fat Man, the Stranger in the house) has effectually stopped the German ships at Cork. It has been one of his most brilliant diplomatic achievements, since he started the concentration camps. I am preparing an answer will hit him in a tender spot.

'The Volunteer movement *can* go only slowly—because we've no money or *officers*. Latter very much needed—their lack is our chief weakness. The raw material is there in plenty—and the spirit. Of course, not being able to arm men makes the drilling, etc., after a time purposeless—so that the thing cannot take on any great extension and will not be alarming to politicians. Besides, what can be said at our harmless and constitutionally aimed movement when nothing has been done for two years against those who have openly and flagrantly organised rebellion and armed resistance to the law? Anything that happens to this Government will be richly deserved—they are contemptible beyond every ordinary British weight and measure. I saw Gill's beard the other night at dinner with your Baron and I behaved scandalously— I could not resist the opportunity to pull it—and I did—and the poor man looked pathetic. He is a real snake—the one Patrick omitted to evict. . . . Redmond's " imperialism " is everywhere repudiated, and by his own supporters, too.

'To expect Irish loyalty to an Empire, still founded on the degradation and spoliation of Ireland, is absurd.

'You know my feelings about the Bill, and its future, has always been the same. I have said, now for two years, and I say it still,

just as assuredly that *this* Bill will never set up a Parliament House
in fact in Ireland. I feel absolutely convinced of it—and nothing
will make me waver.

'The Government *may* pass it on to the Statute Book, in the
course of this Session—that is all they are pledged to do—but it
is, in the interval that follows, before the Parliament can come
into existence, that the Act will be lost.

'I feel convinced in my instinct (which is so frequently a far
truer guide to me than reason or judgment) that this Bill will not
establish a Parliament.

'Where the Liberals have failed is in the long reign of unrestricted power from 1906 to 1910. Then, with the greatest
majority a Government ever had they could have *prepared* the way
for Home Rule by administrative changes in Ireland that rendered it inevitable, and necessary for the mere functions of government. Of course, they'd have had opposition—granted—but *far*
less than to this belated thing—and they were powerful then and
bound in honour to the principles of Home Rule. They ignored
the principles of Home Rule from January, 1906 until 1912-13!
They sent a weakling like Aberdeen—a lampoonist like Birrell—
to go on dealing with Ireland just the same in principle as the
Tories. They could have revolutionised many departments of Irish
Government. They could have separated Ireland *statistically* to
begin with—so as to habituate the minds of this community as a
whole to look at Irish things in their true light as apart from
Great Britain, this could have been done in Customs and in *many
things*: A Treasury Minute upset the Irish Customs in 1823!
A Treasury Minute could have restored many things in 1907-8-9 or
10. They could have *voted* money for administrative needs, so as
to establish an Irish Executive in the country. What have they done
to create any machinery for Irish Government? Absolutely nothing.

'They have allowed Ulster to arm for two years—to *act,* not
merely preach rebellion and open sedition; and when the first
glimmer of manhood begins to show on the side of the unhappy
people they and their long line of predecessors have reduced to
moral, material and economic servitude, they *at once,* within a
week, pervert the law of the U.K. to prohibit the " import " of
arms from abroad—from Great Britain! What liars! For their
own purposes you see, by a stroke of the pen they can create a
separate customs for Ireland! For their own purposes—but never

for our needs. We become, by a mere twist of an Act of Parliament a foreign State, so far as arms and munitions are concerned —even to the searching of baggage of " cross-Channel " passengers. What loyalty can any Irishman with brains and a heart have for *any* English Government? I have none.

' I thank God and Ireland I resigned last June and left their service, for that of my own country and poor, ignorant, demoralised people. If God grants me life and purpose to end as I hope, I'll do some of the things John Mitchel left undone.

' Redmond cannot bind the hearts or pledge the soul of Ireland— they are still living things and will respond to only one touch.

' It will come again—and meantime I do not despair, when I look in the faces of the young men I meet.

' Remember all I told you—for two years now—that *this* Home Rule Bill would not go through. You will see how right I was. They will never put it into *law*. They may pass it, although that I surely doubt too—but it will never grow into a parliament. That, to me, is absolutely clear. . . . Eoin MacNeill writes me that he must give £20 for those documents I spoke of. He is hard at work on the story—and this price must be given the man. I am going to give *him* the £20 today. It must be done. It is for Ireland. . . . Also put up a few prayers for me. For I feel in my bones, I am going to have an awful time of it. But it must be— Fate drives me on. I think the Party themselves are now in their hearts quite in despair of the Bill.

' I had a despairing letter from Cork too on Monday—a man high in the confidence of the Party. He regards all as lost and wrote in despair of the Catholics being driven back into the slough of despond. Poor people—unhappy country—what a fate.

' Don't blame me for my consuming hatred of Shawn Bwee. It is wholly impersonal—just as we are told to hate sin. I *must* fight that iniquity even as I fought Leopold and Arana. British rule in Ireland is an iniquity—a thing to be fought and driven out of the island. If it remains it corrupts, destroys and debauches the people to their final and utter destruction.

' I wish—oh how I wish, I were young—only thirty instead of fifty and with my present knowledge. Eoin MacNeill is full of hope. *All* now (even the most orthodox Nationalists) bless the Volunteers and my Cork friend who denounced them in December now writes that he only regrets there are not more, and that if we "could shoot like the Boers" we'd soon have Home Rule. There is the whole story.

'England surrenders always and only to force. She is surrendering to Ulster, as I have always said she would, because Ulster is prepared to use force—and "wreck the Empire". Ireland is not. Ireland is Catholic, moral and blood-shunning—and so the immoral and blood-delighting win the day.

'There will be a big Volunteer meeting at Dundalk soon. I shall go to it and deliver my soul and say things, I hope, will rouse them all.'

'Meantime all goes well—and the Volunteers are spreading daily. There was a good meeting in Navan on Sunday—and one is coming off at Dundalk in a few days, I hope, at which I am to speak. . . . .

'Ireland looks at one. One sees the question in every living thing—a land and a sea shore waiting for the Deliverer. . . . .

'If we had 100,000 Volunteers ready there would be more than Home Rule offered to Ireland.

'My Kilkenny speech (in the dark, to a tumultuous crowd) I was told last night was the "finest and straightest speech on Nationality delivered in Ireland for years". That is the verdict they said of the Kilkenny men. I am not at all satisfied with it but I've been so occupied with other things I could make no attempt to begin it even until Tuesday last.

'I could not acknowledge the batch of papers before Tuesday— the day I got here after my attempt to break through Carson's bayonets at Craigavon. . . . .

'You know what I've always told you. That *this* government would not do it, and you see I'm right. They've chucked up the sponge to Lord Roberts and company—and the King possibly—and all the criminal conspirators, which is quite right and fitting. English rule in Ireland always has been a criminal conspiracy and it is only right these men should rule to the end by the same methods. Until we can put them out—lock, stock and barrel, Whig and Tory. . . . .

'I was in Belfast—Carson hedged round with bayonets.

'Carson and his 100,000 bluffers are masters of Ulster. . . . And that is why the Bill is dead.

'They may pass it a hundred times on the Statute Book—it is a dead letter over all Ulster until they have settled whether the "Protestant Loyalists" are above or below the law.

' The one outstanding fact for Ireland is this. The Government of Ireland is purely a military Government and never has been anything else. The function of the army is not to defend Ireland but to hold it down in the interests of " England ".

' If called on to assert the rights of an Irish constitution resting on the expressed will of the Irish people, the army declines to enforce the law. It says, quite truly, it is not here for that. It is not here to coerce any but Irish " rebels "—that is its time honoured function and it will not lift a hand except to hold Ireland as a subjugated land—General Gough and company have torn down the sham veil of Constitutional rights of the Irish people and have waved the sabre over our heads as in '98. On both hands we see the appeal, when it comes to the rights of the Irish people, is made to force—naked force. The Ulster Orangemen say *they* are the rulers of Ireland—that England put them here in that capacity and by all their gods they'll stay and maintain their post by force—and when this challenge is taken up by the Government, the Army says the Orangemen are right—and they'll see them through!

' That roughly is the position. Carson said at Dungannon (E. Childers and I heard him) " All Government rests on force: all law rests on force." He is right—and he proceeds to carry it out in practice—and the force that should be on the side of the Irish people, the public forces of the land, say their function is not to support the will of the Irish people, but to maintain the " English garrison " in Ireland. If Ireland will see clearly now that the sham of a British Constitution applying to this land is one of the Master Lies of British Imperial rule, she will have gained greatly from the incident. It is She must meet force with force—and by deliberate preparation, and organisation and sacrifice take her Constitutional rights, and be Mistress in her own house. The more bloodshed the better. The thing would be final. If only we had the manhood and the arms. Alas—the paltry tricksters and schemers will win—and the reign of the bullock will cover all the land—men chewing a cud instead of reflecting—and grazing instead of fighting for their national life.

' I hope to hear from him about the other thing—the serial publication of our exposure—by this mail surely. If he refuses it for the " American " papers—no harm is done—we shall then simply go ahead with it through those publishers.

' I enclose you what may be called one chapter of it—" The Crossmaglen Conspiracy, I." This is derived from another source altogether—not the prime informer. The documents here, too, are appalling. It was this case and the infamy of it drove Trevelyan to fly from Ireland. It dovetails in with the other and larger conspiracy engineered by the whole Cabinet later on. Photographic exposures of leading documents will surely be a part—that we had already decided on. Some of them are masterpieces. " Dear Arthur " will present a fine figure throughout—thank God—also that contemptible animal West Ridgeway—a minor jackal.

' I shall go, I hope, by a German ship about mid-April—just skip without a word when the time comes and by no man seen.

' The influence of England on this unfortunate country is worse today than in any blackest hour of the past. We can never get to think on any single subject now as Irish, or belonging to Ireland.

' Nothing but the external shock can really mend—the earthquake may come—I hope so.'

CHAPTER XII

THE BETRAYAL OF HOME RULE

The great problem still facing them, however, was the almost total absence of arms and ammunition. With the ban on importation, the position seemed hopeless.

On 20th April he attended and spoke at a meeting in Mullingar, and a few days later addressed a large meeting in Tullamore. Here he declared that in Ireland £1,250,000 had been raised for National Insurance, and the same amount if subscribed amongst the people to arm and equip an Irish national army would give the people of Ireland a far better National Insurance.

During these days he wrote : —

' I am under grave suspicion—but the young men of Ireland are more and more my devoted followers.

' Here is a letter from Mitchelstown. Read it. I sent them down at my own cost a colour-sergeant rebel to drill and organise the whole countryside. He is a splendid man and he'll have all the Galteemore and Aherlow and South Tipperary and Cork in six weeks or eight weeks whole-hearted believers in their own manhood.

I am telling him to keep the sergeant at my expense till the whole of the Galtees are drilled and organised.

' At Tullamore tomorrow they propose the four resolutions of the King's Co. Volunteers of 1782. They are, of course, the old strong declaration of national independence. The Party dread and fear me and the Volunteers now—and are trying to capture the latter.'

The lesson of the Curragh affair was not lost on the Orangemen for they now realised that they had a free hand to do as they liked, and that there was no effective power to resist or to control them. Their first move was to send agents to Germany to buy more German arms and ammunition. They succeeded in purchasing there 40,000 German rifles of the Mauser pattern, and an enormous quantity of German rifle cartridges to match. This consignment was paid for in London by cheque, and was shipped from the port of Hamburg to London and transhipped there to a vessel which landed the bulk of the cargo in County Antrim, at the seaport of Larne, and the remainder at Donaghadee. This was carried out as a military operation; the country round Larne was cordoned off by armed Orangemen. Roads were patrolled and the police and coastguard officers were debarred from entry to the town. In compliment to the mutinous General Gough who secured for them this immunity, the password of the day was ' Gough!' This occurred on 24th April, 1914. From that day to this the Orangemen have held, and still hold, these self-same arms, and in consequence have successfully held the north-eastern portion of the national territory.

The position of the great majority of the nation now seemed pretty bleak. Carson and Smith accepted full responsibility for the setting up of this German equipped private army, and openly defied all constitutional authority.

Those Constitutionalists who had believed in Home Rule for Ireland, *i.e.,* the vast majority of the nation, now saw this measure which had been promised to them for years, and which had now passed through all the stages of the legislature, snatched from them by the perfidy of the English Government in secret treaty with the Orange faction. About this time Lord Lansdowne declared in Parliament with frank brutality : ' We have Ireland and we mean to keep her,' and Lord Roberts added that ' military rule over Ireland must be asserted.' These statements were in keeping with what a former military ruler of Ireland, Lord Wolseley, wrote to Queen Victoria: ' The army,' he wrote, ' is not in Ireland to enforce a constitution, but against a hated and despised race.' This same Queen Victoria, urging strong military occupation of Ireland said: ' We must keep there ample forces ready to teach the Irish a lesson or they will begin again.'

The successful manoeuvre by the Curragh military junta in arrangement with the English Government and the Belfast Orangemen dashed the hopes of the nation. In order to rivet the chains still more firmly English troops poured in unceasingly.

It now became quite clear to everyone that the Home Rule Bill which had been dangled before the eyes of the people was just a pious fraud and was merely an English trick to keep the Irish quiet, and the degradation and spoliation of the country was to be continued indefinitely. A very strong feeling of resentment and anger was aroused by the revelation of such contemptible action.

In these desperate straits only one hope remained to the people, namely to concentrate all their efforts to build up a defence force which would be pledged to fight for Irish freedom. The menace and insult to which they were now exposed forced the Irish people to take this measure in self protection.

' If they failed in this duty,' as Casement said, ' they were but a people unworthy of freedom—a dwindling race of cravens from whose veins the blood of manhood had been drained.' He urged at meeting after meeting that every Irishman fit to bear arms in the cause of his country's freedom should do so and should join at once the ranks of the Irish Volunteers.

He wrote from Dublin : —

' I have been here for six days—I came from Belfast on Sunday last to help settle the turmoil. The last three weeks have been bitter and trying. I was ill with influenza since middle of May—on and off and getting worse, and then came the " Crisis."

' The resolution to call on the thirty-two counties to elect Volunteer delegates was mine, and arrived at *prior* to Mr. R.'s first letter of 10th June. The night before. Such a tragedy. I came up from Belfast specially on 9th June (the Tuesday) and put down that resolution and got a special meeting called to discuss it for the Friday —and came here with Eoin MacN. that night, the 9th. I wrote to Redmond and begged him to exercise goodwill and dismiss distrust, and I posted it at 1 a.m. (in time for the morning boat) and went to bed—hoping that I had saved the situation. In the morning (Wednesday, 10th June) appeared his truculent letter. I wired him. The special meeting for Friday then became an extra special for Wednesday (that night) and at it we voted my resolution of the previous night—the 32 elected delegates from the Volunteers—as the best reply to Mr. Redmond. I wrote him the next day, Thursday (very briefly from bed ill here) to say that it furnished him with every guarantee, etc., etc.

' His reply was extremely curt, saying I had " doubtless " seen his letter of 10th June to which, " of course," he adhered. Then came his letter of Saturday, 20th—to which we replied by Tuesday night's " surrender." I drafted the surrender mostly—it was Bulmer Hobson's suggestion. The sworn enemy of the Party. Eoin MacN. and I and Col. Moore had decided to resign in a body rather than split the country, and to state that the Irish Volunteers as " originally constituted " had ceased to exist—but Bulmer came on the Monday and implored me to reconsider that suggestion and adopt the one we ultimately took. His argument was that no appeal to honour or patriotism would have any effect on these men—that if we resigned we simply handed the Volunteer movement over to Redmond and the Hibernians and Dillon, etc., lock, stock and barrel. Better wait, keep as firm a hold as possible on the wheel—and once " Home Rule " is out of the way we could act independently. I gave in to this view—so did Eoin, and Col. Moore will say ditto to anything we suggest. So we drew up that statement—all three of us ill (for they, too, had influenza) and carried it (with great difficulty and many heart-burnings) at the Tuesday night's meeting. It was a tragic meeting. Tom Kettle proved himself an utter blackguard and got the reception of a lifetime.

' We could have rent the country and split it into two camps— Young Ireland versus Old England. I got pledges of support from the West—and others. Many thousands, in fact, all the real Volunteers—apart from the Party men and the Catholic Party who want defence against Protestants (i.e., in the Ulster counties) would have followed us. We should have been the Volunteers versus the " Irish Party "—and Home Rule would assuredly have been wrecked—no less than the Volunteers. All would have gone under. I pointed this out and said that for the sake of the country, and for its sake only, I accepted Mr. R's suggestion. We, the majority (it was carried by

18 to nine), are, of course, naturally attacked bitterly by the extremists or the " principle " men. The " principle " might have been saved—but nothing else. Out of the raging faction fight would have emerged a disgraced Ireland with no Home Rule and no Volunteers. That was clear to me. It was for the sake of this poor distracted country and *to* this poor distracted country, on what I know to be its wish, I surrendered. Not to that contemptible gang of tricksters and liars at Westminster, with the new Pope of Swinford in the chair. That miserable humbug, Dillon—see the insolence of the enclosed letter to Swinford. I thought of challenging him to make good his cowardly insinuations—charges by innuendo—but feel it is better at present to keep quiet. They will soon be in such disfavour over the impending debacle of " Home Rule " that one can " wait and see " with a vengeance.

' I am thoroughly wretched in many ways. I know we did the right thing. But it has caused me despair. The cause of Ireland seems so hopeless in the hands of such men. How can any freedom arise in the land with such a narrow-minded, intolerant bigot as John Dillon, tool and agent of English Liberalism—and Joe Devlin —ignorant, forceful, greedy, ambitious, wielder of mob oratory and organiser of machine-made opinion—as the leaders? Redmond is in the hands of these men and of T. P. O'C. The letter was actually written by O'Connor. The country *is* being sold—for place and posts and profit—into the hands of the English. I feel it and see it proceeding. These men do not want Irish freedom—they want merely majority rule, i.e., Catholic rule in Ireland—and under it England will more and more strangle Ireland and emasculate the minds of the people. I feel like going for good—what can one do? To be unselfish and want nothing for yourself is *the* crime with these scoundrels. Why, they tried to tempt Eoin MacN. by a carefully-worded offer of place and profit. As for me—they know me too well. I have only horror for them—and pity, sorrow and compassion for this poor, faithful, affectionate, generous-hearted people always betrayed by their own weakness and inability to differentiate between the true and the sham true. To label this wretched travesty of " self government " " the restoration of national independence " —as the Party does daily—is accepted by the people as a true label.

' I am, candidly, more and more feeling that the destruction of the Bill may be the best thing for Ireland. It will end *forever* this dependence on lies from Westminster. This is the Party's last chance and they know it.

'I think they also know that the Bill is doomed—and this rumpus over the Volunteers was deliberately got up in order to put the blame for the failure of "Home Rule" on the "factionists." Dillon let that cat out of the bag two weeks ago at Ballaghadereen.

'Redmond is so little patriotic at heart that he left the whole fate of the Home Rule Bill in *our* hands. Just think of it. They knew and had publicly stated so—that the *only* thing that could now snatch the cup of liberty from the lips of Ireland was "indiscipline in the ranks of the national army" (Dillon's words). They take that dreadful risk. They knew that had we rejected their terms and appealed to our principles and to the young men to stand by us, we should have rent Ireland in twain—in every county, town and parish in Ireland.

'And they knew that if this arose Home Rule was chucked on the scrap heap. And they took that risk. So that we have shown a far higher patriotism than theirs—for we sacrificed ourselves, our ideal, our reputations, even with those whose regard we cherish—to save a Bill none of us think much of—for the sake of the country and its fixed desire to get Home Rule. What a disillusionment it will be when they get it—and find they have got a debating society on the banks of the Liffey with Joe Devlin and John Dillon throttling every aspiration, quenching every hope of the heart of the people.

'Anyhow, I am finished with the Provisional Committee—and I only wait until "Home Rule" is settled to revive the cause of Young Ireland.'

CHAPTER XIII

IRISH CITIZENS MASSACRED IN DUBLIN

It was not, however, until some months later that he had a limited success when in co-operation with the Irish Volunteers 1,500 rifles were landed at Howth from the yacht of the late Mr. Erskine Childers; a yacht in which he had sailed to Hamburg for the purpose of buying these guns. Far different, however, was the British reaction to this incident compared to what happened in the landing of 40,000 rifles in Antrim by the Orangemen a few months previously. A regiment of the King's Own Scottish Borderers was despatched at once to Howth to seize the landed arms, but on the way they got the worst of a skirmish with the Volunteers and promptly abandoned the attempt. This regiment then marched back to Dublin much discomfited at being out-manoeuvred and showed their chagrin by opening fire indiscrimin-ately on, and bayoneting the civilian population in the Dublin streets. They killed and wounded numbers of men, women and children. The date of this occurrence was July 26th, 1914, a few days before the outbreak of World War I.

Having set in motion this enterprise for a first consignment of arms Casement had left for the United States on 4th July, 1914, in order to obtain a further supply. As he was now being carefully watched by secret service agents he booked a second class passage from Glasgow to Montreal where he arrived on the 16th and on following day left for New York. In a very short time he was in deep consultations with the Irish-American leaders, John Devoy, Bourke Cochran, John Quinn and Joseph McGarrity. On July 26th he wrote from Philadelphia :

' This war that has come like a bombshell from the Almighty arsenal may throw *everything* into the fire. If Germany is involved as seems most likely, John Bull *will have* to face the music—whether he likes it or not—and then. . . .

' *All* here without exception almost are against Redmond's surrender to Ulster and a very little thing now would rout the Party irrecoverably with the Irish in America.

' Devoy speaks for the great majority I think—and it is absurd for Redmond to claim that he has the Irish here behind him. Why, I *could* put him out of court in two weeks here if I liked to play that game. They crowded round me at Norfolk and many more came privately and said : " You are the man we want." They are sick of talk and Parliamentarianism and will give their strength and hearts only to some leader who will fight.

' John Devoy said he had heard from you—but your letter had of course been opened and read. The spy system here is profound. We have ample proof of it. He does not want to write back to you on that account.

' So please keep guard—and in all things now the *fewer* who know anything the better. We are surrounded by spies. Every

British Embassy, Legation and Consulate here has a staff of paid spies and informers at work—recreant Irishmen. Many are after me now. All letters are got at some way or other and the U.S.A. Government of Wilson is pro-British and would help.

'The fight over Panama has revealed the *strength* of the Irish. They have shown the whole country that they are the best Americans in it and have got a stronger footing than ever.

'At Norfolk, Virginia, when the two-yearly Convention of the Hibernians was held, the whole town was *en fête* for the Irish. It was wonderful and uplifting.

'*Everywhere* the Irish flag in the place of honour and only it and the Stars and Stripes. No other flags of any kind and these two with the green in the middle and on high festooning and arching all the main streets and buildings—all the taxicabs covered with Irish flags.

'Everywhere goodwill for the Irish—admiration for them and expressions of the highest regard for their character, their manliness and good faith. It is a revelation to me—they are a *great people* and one has to come to America to see what they are capable of. The editors of all the papers I've been interviewed by are keen friends of Ireland and loud in their goodwill.

'Remember—any more picnics *must* be run by only two or three caterers at outside. Bringing in others opens the door to the gang always on the watch.

'If this war breaks out as seems likely then be prepared for *everything*. God knows what may come from it—*all* I have predicted of which you know—may come, or be attempted. I am waiting hourly for a telegram today from Ireland to say the picnic has been held or prevented, or broken up. Today was the day of Fate.'

When he learned by telegram that the rifles had been successfully landed at Howth, he was overjoyed and wrote to Dublin.

29 July, 1914.

'How can I tell you all I have felt since Sunday. I can never tell you. I was in anguish first—then filled with joy—and now with a resolute pride in you all. We have done what we set out to do. And done it well. The Irish here are mad with anger but filled with pride, joy and hope. All else is swept aside in these feelings—old J.D. says with a glow of joy "the greatest deed done in Ireland for 100 years" and keeps on repeating it.

' We have struck a blow for Ireland which will echo round the world. Were it not for the stupendous war cloud the Press here would be filled—as it is they give much—although they are a *bad Press*. A real bad *Press*—uninstructed, fumbling, stupid and unenlightened on everything but baseball, American finance and politics. Their " interviews " are ineptitude condensed.

' May the gods of Erin put rifles into the arms of Irishmen and teach them to shoot straight. My grief is that I was here and not on the Howth Road last Sunday and my blood is hot with wrath when I think of that bayoneting and bulleting—but God bless you and all who helped this noble gift of arms and those two Irish lads who shipped as hands aboard. May this bring a new day to Ireland—I see it coming—new hope, new courage on the old, old manhood.'

CHAPTER XIV

NEW YORK. PUBLIC MEETINGS AND SECRET CONFERENCES

Although he had evaded the English spies when he quietly slipped away from Dublin his movements were now closely watched in New York. A week later England declared war on Germany and at once commenced a vigorous recruiting campaign in Ireland with the full support of the Redmondite party. This party had become the mere tail of the Liberal Party and its nationalism was little more than a political catch-cry.

On August 15th he wrote from New York : —

' The New York Press is filled with lies against Germany. The Carnegie graft money has not been spent in vain these last six years! Poor Germany! My heart bleeds for those poor people beset by a world of hatred, envy and jealousy. Their crime is their efficiency. England is playing an atrocious part. All I prophesied to you you see has come—but oh! so soon. England will pay dearly for this in the end—*her* fate is sealed. She wins, perhaps, today by the sword of Russia and France—not by her own manhood! And the sword she has hired to slay German commerce and industry will yet be turned against her in the East. For this vile and cowardly Government of liars, oh! what contempt I have—and to think of Ireland dragged at their heels to aid in assassinating the one great, free people of Europe whose virtues, industry and sobriety they feared.

' Redmond has lost the faith of all Irish here—they spit his name out of their mouths. I am well—do all you can to help my poor old sister.

' The Irish here are fine—and I am not in despair—yet. I feel that there must be some Almighty power will assert its might for good—and that this threat to mankind, to be ruled by Russian brute force and English cunning and greed for fifty years will be met by some great deed of manhood.

' If Germany wins through against this league of criminals hope shall spring again. If she goes under I despair indeed. Lost opportunities are the tombstones of nations and great causes—and I see where some have come and not been used.

' I don't see anything clear. It is a ruined old world I see—and English conspiracy triumphant. This is England's war—she has plotted it and planned it for years and it is *her silent* pledging of herself to France and Russia that has brought on the attack. History will put the crime on the right shoulders.

' I would I were young—I should know what to do: but I feel broken and old and I see the evil powers are again winning. God bless and keep you—for Ireland's sake—and mine.'

On September 14th he wrote from New York:

' Up to the 5th September I had some hope—but the rout from Paris of the great advance kills hope. I see the doom of Germany—I have, indeed, seen it all along—but there was hope while the advance went on. Now the beasts of prey will have the corpse—or, rather, the hyaena will. . . .

' England will take our foodstuffs, just as she will take our young men for her own greedy gains. *We* have no men to spare to fight the English battle of robbing Germany of her trade and destroying her navy. Even did any of the profit or plunder of the defeated race come to Ireland, I should still, as an Irishman, oppose the war on grounds of national morality. It is a conspiracy against the *one* people in Europe England feared for their virtues, not for their faults. It is not " German militarism " angers her or that she has joined the two mercenary bullies, Russia and France, in assailing—

but German *anti-militarism*—German commerce, German industry, German naval efficiency and seamanship. There would have been and *could* have been no war now but for England. She as surely made this war as she did the Boer war—and for exactly the same end. The whole game for years has been, " *When* and How." I have heard it discussed again and again in the Foreign Office, and the game there was to deceive Germany—I shall never willingly set foot on English soil again or harbour friendship for the race or country. They are cowards and assassins at heart. Witness Lord Curzon's speech of vilification of the German Emperor the other day—and the daily jeers and jibes telegraphed over here of English " gentlemen."

'Well, I can't tell you *anything* about myself—because I expect this letter will be opened.

'John Bull is trying all he can to corral the States, and if he gets one naval defeat (as may well occur) he is going to put up a howl for " Anglo-Saxon solidarity."

'The British authorities here are spending money like water. Spies everywhere! The latest piece of strategy is gangs of "boosters" hired to go out round the newspaper offices and cheer for " little Belgium." Gangs of public-house loafers are engaged secretly at the Consulate-General and invest the notice boards when the news is given out. I sent two off with roars of laughter, on Saturday, from the crowd, and they retreated discreetly.

'The opening of all German letters on neutral ships; the seizing of neutral ships and taking off of any passengers they "suspect"; the constant violations of neutrality here by England in sending out messages and supplies to her warships—and the barefaced lying going on in the U.S.A. Press on her behalf—are the most sickening exhibitions of her innate cowardice. She is not satisfied with having got Russia, France, Belgium, Servia and Japan on the backs of the Germanic peoples—but she would dearly like to have the Americans, the Italians and the brave Balkanites.

'I send you some literature—I wonder if it will reach you. *No. 1* is printed 50,000 here and gone all over the land—and to all Government and Parliament men and universities. *No.* 2 is a broadsheet; will make you laugh. No. 3 is an item of the Irish Press Bureau output.

'P. Colum and wife called on Saturday on their way to Pittsburg with latest news. (No. 1, by the way, is being sold in the streets by

Sisters of Charity distributing bread in Dublin during the Easter Week Insurrection, 1916.

Dublin after the artillery bombardment by the British during Easter Week, 1916.

the newsboys—and the British " boosters " get very angry when they see it being bought.)

' There is not much good in my going back. Feeling as I do about this war of cowardice and greed, how could I keep silent. I am *bound* to speak out and to pray my country to abstain. That should be done in any case by some of the Provisional Committee. It is monstrous that in this downfall of all national feeling and morality no man should stand out to say at all costs where Ireland's honour, duty and morality lead. If I return—I say it openly and at once—at least, if we cannot fight for our soul we can plead for it.

' The poor Germans! God help them—" God save Germany " I pray night and day. She is going to her doom—the Hyaena waiting for the corpse, to be killed to corpsedom by the Bear and the Polecat and the Tigercat and a few more fighting pets—with the Hyaena prowling round the outside, *waiting for the Corpse*. Oh! how I long for a chance to strike a blow as the Irish did at Fontenoy, and there are thousands here the same! Had we a war chest we could get the Hyaena some new spots. But God in *some* day will do that—and, probably Russia will be the paymaster. When the Anglo-Saxon corpse comes it will not be so brave a fight or so fine a corpse as the Teuton one of today—God save Germany. . . . .

' It is the Emperor's fault. I have heard the whole story here from the highest quarter—the Emperor *believed* in England, was bent on winning England, determined to have her goodwill and friendship and then, through that, to come to terms of amity with France. He would allow nothing to be said or done to hurt England or English susceptibilities—and this is the result! This is the gratitude. His friendship for England has brought this great country and people to the very threshold of calamity—and I see nothing but a miracle that can save them. I fear the miracle won't operate—and that Germany will go down for 40 or 50 years. England will be supreme —as I warned Roosevelt. He grinned and said: " *She* won't— *because she's finished.*" I laughed and said: " You are wrong—she will swell to bigger things yet and in the end inoculate *you* with the virus of her own disease! You will become imperialists and join her in the plunder of the earth." So it will be—as surely as that the sun shines and that *is* the fate reserved for mankind until some other race—maybe Tartar or Japanese or Russian, starts a new form of imperialist that shall put the Anglo-Saxon one, built on commercial greed, out of business. The triumph of Germany would have meant healthy competition and a play of forces and a true " balance of power "—that phrase that England fights for! She means by balance of power no one in a position to challenge her supremacy of the seas and impair her appetite for more.

' If I come while the war is on I shall be in jail within a week, or in a concentration camp, or in flight to the hills—I can't and won't keep quiet and allow the soul of the land to be drugged.'

' I know the stream of atrocious lies that is flooding Ireland—to get Irish boys entrapped into the army in defence of the religion —the nuns, priests, etc., outraged by the German savages. The time has come when if we can do nothing else, we should go to jail.

' I will come and join and go to jail gladly. I begin today with a public protest here to John Bull Redmond's shameful appeal on behalf of the other Bull.

' If Asquith and his ally come to Dublin they should be shot— were I at home I'd do it. I trust someone will. It is said by hundreds of Irishmen here.

' Tell the Professor he and the other Provincial Committee men who are true should issue a proclamation against joining the army —add my name too—and I'll come and face the music. Put it on grounds of Christian duty as well as of patriotism and public morality—and add any treason your heart dictates.'

Casement was not for a moment deceived by the pretence that England had declared war in order to save small nations from oppression; he realised that the English attack was designed to crush a serious trade rival whose industry and technical genius was then threatening England's virtual monopoly of the world's industrial markets. In a letter written from New York and published in Dublin on 17th September, he wrote:

' As an Irishman and one who has been identified with the Irish Volunteer movement since it began, I feel it my duty to protest against the claim now put forward by the British Government, that, because it has agreed with its political opponents " to place the Home Rule Bill on the statute book," and to defer the operation until after the war, and until an " Amending Bill " to profoundly amend its provisions has been introduced and passed, Irishmen in return should enlist in the British Army and aid the Allied Asiatic and European powers in a war against a people who have never wronged Ireland. The British Liberal Party has been publicly pledged for 28 years to give self government to Ireland. It has not yet fulfilled that pledge . . . . Ireland has no quarrel with the German people or just cause of offence against them.

' I will not pronounce an opinion upon the British standpoint in this war, beyond saying that the public profession under which it began, namely to defend the violated neutrality of Belgium, is being daily controverted by the official spokesmen of Great Britain.

' Ireland had no blood to give to any land, to any cause, but that of Ireland. Our duty as a Christian people is to abstain from bloodshed; and our duty as Irishmen is to give our lives for Ireland. Ireland needs all her sons.

' Ireland has suffered at the hands of British administration a more prolonged series of evils, deliberately inflicted, than any other community of civilised men; . . . .

' If Irish bloodshed is to be " the seal that will bring all Ireland together in one nation and in liberties equal and common to all " then let that blood be shed in Ireland, where alone it can be righteously shed to secure those liberties. It was not Germany destroyed the national liberties of the Irish people, and we cannot recover the national life struck down in our own land by carrying fire and sword into another land.

' The cause of Ireland is greater than that of any party; higher than the worth of any man; richer in its poverty than all the riches of Empire. If we sell it now we are unworthy of the name of Irishmen. If today we barter that cause in a sordid bargain, we shall prove ourselves a people unworthy of freedom. . . . . If now to fight is our duty, then let us fight on that soil where so many generations of slain Irishmen lie in honour and fame. Let our graves be in that patriot grass whence alone the corpse of Irish nationality can spring to life. Ireland will be false to her history, to every consideration of honour, good faith and self-interest if she now willingly responds to the call of the British Government to send her brave sons and faithful hearts to fight in a cause that has no glint of chivalry or gleam of generosity in all its line or battle. If this be a war for the " small nationalities," as its planners term it, then let it begin, for one small nationality, at home.'

Casement well knew the extreme difficulty of getting arms for he wrote :

' I think it will be easier to get them from U.S.A.—but it is already a task of great difficulty with England so supreme at sea and Ireland ringed round with ships, enemies—and spies.'

In the war of the Boer Republic in defence of its independence, an Irishman named Major John MacBride raised, with some others, an Irish Brigade to fight on her side. He was taken prisoner by the British forces while fighting in the Irish Rising in 1916, put against the barrack wall and shot by a platoon of English soldiers. Casement now formed the idea of forming an Irish Brigade from the Irishmen who had been recruited into the British Army, and had later been captured and made prisoners in Germany. That he got this idea from Major MacBride is clear from the letter quoted on page 100.

He also set himself the task of getting arms from the only possible remaining source—Germany.

He put these suggestions to the German Ambassador, Count von Bernstorff, who was so impressed with them that he sent word to the Foreign Office in Berlin that Casement would be going over there shortly. In a letter to an Irish friend from New York, 11th October, 1914, he wrote:

' It takes blood and iron to make nations as well as Empires. The century of persistent talk substituted for work has wrought Ireland almost irreparable injury—that, and a vicious administration bent on debauching, demoralising, estranging and exploiting an emigrant race has come near to well-nigh destroying the country and debarring it any possible future save that of a cattle ranch.

' The Home Rule Administration, if it comes, will be more surely a London administration than even Dublin Castle today I fancy. All the " leaders " are now so deeply committed to British policies and English politics that they will be handed over the administration of Dublin Castle only on the clear provision that it shall be on lines favourable to English interests. What those interests are we know—and they do not include a prosperous, self-respecting or self-reliant Ireland of live men.

' I sent you some copies of my Manifesto. I think it is honest. I wrote it straight from the heart, on reading those repellent speeches of Asquith, Crewe, etc., etc., and then Redmond's appeal of treachery to our poor, faithful, brave boys to go out to die for England's pillage of the German markets.

'One thing is clear. We must try to keep the youth at home. From no possible point of view is it right or good they should go to France or Flanders in this accursed upheaval of hell abroad.

'Sir E. Grey should be hanged *far* higher than Haman. Of all the villainous fools British greed of Empire has yet produced that wicked, stupid, obstinate fool is the worst. The tool of a gang of unscrupulous anti-Germans (Tyrrell, Cartwright, King Edward, Bertie, Delcasse, etc., etc.) he as surely committed his country to this war as Czar, Kaiser, or any other autocrat—and yet the horrid things pose to the world as a " democracy ". Fancy a democracy run by Sir Wm. Tyrrell!

'The war is all I call it—and far more. We see more of it here than you do. You get only the British lies—we get them too, but some of the other lies also—or truths.

'What you should bear in mind, for Ireland and her future is this—this is one thing should not be lost sight of. All the arguments proceed on the fixed assumption that England must be victorious and Germany beaten—except when, for recruiting purposes, they try to scare Ireland by painting the awful picture of a " German invasion "—or of " a defeated British Empire and Ireland prostrate at the foot of the conqueror!"

'Why should Ireland incur the possible injury that *may* come to Great Britain? The latter has *never* shared her gains or goods with Ireland—only her disasters. *She* counts on our always giving her of *all* we have—what has she given us in return? Let us be wise and prudent today—*and keep every Irish boy and man in Ireland*.

'I see a side of this world war that is hidden from you in those little islands.

'I see this one thing very clearly. The immediate and vital issue for Ireland is to keep her hands clean. To keep her conscience clean. This war is no concern of hers. It is *England's* war for sea supremacy and world trade against a people who have no thought of hurting us in their hearts, heads or plans—unless, like the Belgians, we willingly play the game of their enemies. A large " Irish army " in the field against Germany will be the climax to our woes—a gratuitous gift of our last blood to a bad cause.

'England cannot hurt us more than she has done—and we

shall be better able to protect ourselves if we keep our blood at home to use for our own ruined industries and trade. Germany, *today* has no wish or thought of hurting Ireland—but if we go out as Redmond and Asquith want, then obviously and quite rightly she will be called on to deal with us just as any other of the enemies assailing her if she should win through. And she is by no means beaten. Remember that. She may even win—at worst conclude a very honourable peace.

' We should look beyond the present. This war will have bitter memories, new animosities, future hatreds. Let Ireland avoid all. Let her stay in her cabbage garden and try and keep the children safe. That is about all we can do. My policy is not mean or paltry —it is wise. It is the *only* way we have today of asserting our nationality—and the *only* way of perhaps safeguarding it.

' We have no quarrel with Germany—no righteous cause of strife with her. To war upon her at the bidding of England is unrighteous, immoral, and a crime against our national life and perhaps our very vital existence. We have a legal, a moral right to abstain. Let us abstain.

' Should England be beaten—as she richly deserves to be for her criminal conspiracy against Germany—let *her* pay the cost. We should be safe. I know whereof I talk. I have, perhaps, done more for Irish safety (and Irish virtue too for that matter) than you will ever know.

' Anyhow it is a wicked lie to say as they are saying at home that the Germans would ravage, plunder and pillage in Ireland. There is no possibility of their getting there or remote likelihood of it but to-day *we* out here have secured their goodwill, their gratitude and even their affection and rest assured of this—these factors count always in human affairs. We have made a pact of friendship here in America and if Ireland at home will only keep to her own green fields, attend to her own business, keep her volunteers *in Ireland* and keep them straight and staunch to the ideal of their foundation we shall have done all that is humanly possible in a crisis of human affairs.'

Chapter XV

CASEMENT OUTWITS THE SPY RING. SAILS FOR NORWAY

There were, however, many difficulties to be overcome to make the passage. Casement's hotel was beset with spies and his every movement closely observed. At length, he decided on a plan to outwit his guards. Through the efforts of his Irish-American friends he obtained a passport made out in the name of a gentleman whom he would impersonate. To carry his papers and luggage he engaged as a servant a Norwegian named Adler Christensen, a man whom he had befriended soon after arriving in New York. For him he booked a second class passage to his home town at Moss, Norway. Casement now moved to a hotel where he registered as ' Mr. R. Smythe,' while at the same time his Irish friends booked rooms for him at the La Salle Hotel, Chicago, and published press notices in the Chicago papers of his expected arrival there in two days. Having sent Christensen down to the ship, Casement shaved off his beard, and left the hotel by a side door, and by this ruse he succeeded in throwing the watchers off the track.

Accompanied by the Irish-American whom he was personating, and whose passport he carried, he went on board, with Christensen as his servant.

The Irish-American slipped quietly ashore, and then at 2 p.m., October 15th, Casement was launched on his perilous journey to Berlin via Christiania.

Posing as an American was no easy matter, and with three real Americans on board he had some difficulty in explaining his Irish accent. However as most, if not all, the passengers were travelling under assumed names and false passports, it ill became them to enquire into those of the others on board. On Thursday, the 22nd October, it was noted by all that the ship had taken a more northern course, although this did not appear on the ship's chart. Two days later, off the Faröe Islands, they were halted by an English cruiser, and this was the signal for Casement to conceal or throw overboard any incriminating papers or documents in his possession. Into Stornoway then the ' Oskar II ' was taken, and there was not a man on the ship who was not convinced that Casement had given the signal to the cruiser, and that he was in reality an English agent. As a result of the search six arrests were made, and then the ship resumed its journey, and arrived at Christiania on 28th October.

CHAPTER XVI

ATTEMPTED MURDER IN CHRISTIANIA

Here Casement engaged rooms at the Grand Hotel, which was to be the scene of the notorious attempt on his life by the English Ambassador, Findlay. In order to obtain his permit for admission to Germany Casement, after some shopping in the Christiania streets, attended at the German Legation where he presented his letter of introduction from Count Bernstorff to the German Minister in Norway, Count von Oberndorff. As this letter was in code, Casement was asked to return next day for the necessary papers. While in the streets Casement noticed a man following him and watching his movements. His suspicions were confirmed later when Christensen informed him that a stranger speaking fluent Norwegian had got into conversation with him and invited him to 79 Drammenavein, where he was greeted by another Norwegian who pressed him with questions about the ' tall dark gentleman ' who was staying at the hotel, and who had arrived on the ' Oskar II ' from America. When Casement heard this and found on looking up the street directory that the address was that of the British Legation, he immediately informed the German Ambassador whom he saw the same evening at 7 o'clock. On their way to keep the appointment the taxi was followed at a respectable distance by a car, the occupant of which both Casement and Christensen recognised to be the inquisitive stranger. By leaving the taxi in a side street, and proceeding on foot to the Embassy, Casement succeeded in evading his pursuer, realising his danger on account of holding a false passport. In the interview with Count von Oberndorff he urged the necessity for speed in issuing the required papers for admission into Germany. Later the same evening in the hotel, an attempt was made to bribe Christensen with a twenty dollar gold piece to give some information about his employer. Perturbed about this incident Casement determined to leave Christiania and attempt to enter Germany even without the diplomatic papers. At midnight, however, the secretary of the German Legation called to say that the permit was on the way. Next morning early he saw from his window, an observer posted intently watching the hotel from across the street, and he was greatly relieved when Mr. Hilmers, the secretary of the Legation, called to say that the papers would be ready later that day. Meanwhile a scribbled message was passed to Christensen in the hotel lounge, which read : ' Phone 11,460 and you will hear something good '; when he did so he was told to come to the British Legation by taxi. On this occasion he was brought into the presence of Mr. M. Findlay, the English Ambassador, who put him through a thorough cross-examination, and broadly hinted that Casement was endeavouring to obtain German help for the Irish against England; that he was a dangerous man, and then suggested that ' as Casement was in Norway under an assumed name if he could be made to disappear no one would know, because there was no one to make enquiries after a person that does not exist.' Continuing, Findlay said to Christensen : ' Suppose this gentleman were knocked on the head it would be a very good thing for him who did it.' After some bargaining Findlay offered £5,000 for this commission to which Christensen pretended to agree.

While Christensen was then occupied in this ' negotiation,' Casement had engaged a berth in a sleeping-car to Copenhagen and gave as a forwarding address the Hotel Bristol, Copenhagen. On making enquiries at the station, it was found that the train to Copenhagen was in two sections, one bound for Copenhagen and the other for the frontier town of Sassnitz. In order to put his pursuers off the scent, immediately on Christensen's return to the hotel he ordered him to put the luggage and engage seats in the Copenhagen section. When, however, they reached the junction town of Engleholm they transferred rapidly into the other section and watched the Copenhagen section leave the platform carrying with it an agent from the British Legation who had followed them in the train. The train took them to Traelleborg, where they embarked on the railway steamer for a five hour trip to Sassnitz on the German frontier. Beyond some minor passport difficulties there, the travellers reached Berlin without incident on the evening of 31st

October, and put up at the Continental Hotel. Mr. Richard Meyer, a brother of the famous Celtic scholar, Dr. Kuno Meyer, who had accompanied Casement from Christiania, was of great assistance on the journey. As a further kindness on the following day he went to the Foreign Office and made an appointment with the Under Secretary of State, Herr Zimmermann. It transpired that the Chancellor, Bethmann-Hollweg, and the Secretary of State, Herr von Jagow, were both at this time with the Emperor at Charleville on the Western Front.

Chapter XVII

BERLIN. GERMANY DECLARES FOR IRISH FREEDOM

At the appointed time Casement attended at the Foreign Office where he was received by Herr Zimmermann and afterwards by Count Georg von Wedel. Recording the thoughts and hopes which passed through his mind while waiting, he wrote :

' Strange thoughts were mine, as I sat on a big sofa in this centre of policy of the German Empire. No regrets, no fears— well, yes, some regrets, but no fears. I thought of Ireland, the land I should almost fatally never see again. Only a miracle could ever bring me to her shores. That I did not expect—cannot in truth hope for. But, victory or defeat, it is all for Ireland, and she cannot suffer from what I do. I may, I must suffer—and even those near and dear to me—but my country can only gain from my treason. Whatever comes that must be so. If I win it is national resurrection —a free Ireland, a world nation after centuries of slavery. A people lost in the Middle Ages refound and returned to Europe. If I fail—if Germany be defeated—still the blow struck today for Ireland must change the course of British policy towards that country. Things will never be quite the same. The " Irish Question " will have been lifted from the mire and mud and petty, false strife of British domestic politics into an international atmosphere. That, as least, I shall have achieved. England can never again play with the " Irish Question ". She will *have* to face the issue once for all. With the clear issue thus raised by me she will have to deal. She must either face a discontented, conspiring Ireland—or bind it closer by a grant of far fuller liberties. Coercion she cannot again resume. *Laissez-faire* must go forever. "Home Rule" must become indeed Home Rule—and even if all my hopes are doomed to rank failure abroad, at least I shall have given more to Ireland by one bold deed of open treason than Redmond and Company after years of talk and spouting treason have gained from England. England does not mind the "treason" of the orthodox Irish "patriot". She took the measure of that long ago. She only fears the Irishman who *acts*; not him who talks. She recognises only action, and respects only deeds. Those men have killed England with their mouth time and again —I am going to hit her with my clenched hand. It is a blow of sincere enmity, based on a wholly impersonal disregard of consequences to myself. Sure alone that it is in truth a blow for Ireland I *should* be a traitor did I not act as I am doing. I have often said, and said it without the slightest concealment, that if ever the chance came to strike a blow for Ireland *I'd* do it. Well, the chance has come. I am not responsible for it. The crime is not mine. It is England's own doing. Grey and Asquith are the real traitors. They have surely betrayed *their* country and her true interests to glut the greedy jealousy of the British commercial mind. Germany's sin has been her efficiency. They chose to build up a league of enmity against the people they feared to assail themselves, and having triumphed in their tortuous, ignoble secret diplomacy they joyfully hurried to the encounter when, at last, sure as they thought of their prey. For them, that so-called Liberal Administration I have nothing but unmeasured contempt. A scorn I cannot express. And for the "governing classes" too of the pirate realm. For the people themselves, and for many individual Englishmen, I have only deep sorrow, regret, pity and affection. But as Wilfred Blunt said to me in Sussex at Newbuildings, in May when I lunched with him and that lovely girl (the great-grand-daughter of Lord Edward Fitzgerald)—the time has come for the break-up of the British Empire.

'Even as he said he hoped *now* to live to see it, so I hope to be able to *do* something to bring it about. That Empire is a monstrosity.'

During the interview he submitted a memorandum which outlined a form of declaration which he suggested the German Government should issue to the press; a declaration expressing

officially the attitude of the German Government towards Ireland.
With this memorandum Zimmermann expressed his thorough
agreement and then spoke in the most cordial terms of German
goodwill and support for Irish national aspirations. In the interview
with Count von Wedel Casement introduced his proposal to form
an Irish Brigade from the Irish prisoners then in German hands
whom he hoped to organise to fight for the freedom of their country.
He said:

'I made it plain beyond all misconception to Wedel that my
efforts with the soldiers must be strictly defined as an effort to strike
a blow for Ireland—not an attempt merely to hit England.'

His mission closely resembled that of Theobald Wolfe Tone, who
in 1796 had come from America with letters from the French
Ambassador, one addressed to the American Ambassador and another
in code to the French Government outlining Tone's mission to
obtain military aid for his country. Both Tone and Casement succeeded in their missions but failed to get the arms landed in Kerry
as they hoped. In the end they were both captured on landing in
Ireland and were both judicially murdered.

In the course of the official German declaration which followed
Casement's representations the following lines occur:

'The Imperial Government formally declares that under no circumstances would Germany invade Ireland with a view to its
conquest or the overthrow of any native institutions in that country.

'Should the fortune of this great war, that was not of Germany's
seeking, ever bring in its course German troops to the shores of
Ireland, they would land there, not as an army of invaders to pillage
and destroy, but as the force of a Government that is inspired by
goodwill towards a country and a people for whom Germany desires
only national prosperity and national freedom.'

Casement wrote at this time to Eoin MacNeill:

'The enemy is doing everything to keep the truth out of Ireland,
and are even trying to get the Vatican on their side, as in the time
of Parnell. Once our people, clergy and volunteers know that
Germany, if victorious, will do her best to aid us in our efforts to
achieve an independent Ireland, every man at home must stand for
Germany and Irish freedom.'

About this time he met an old friend who had been in Africa
with him—Count Gebhard Blücher and they had many pleasant
evenings together.

On the 18th December, 1914, Count von Wedel of the Foreign Office took him to the Ministry for an interview with the Chancellor, Bethmann-Hollweg. The Chancellor stated that he was in thorough agreement with Casement's idea of a free and independent Ireland and listened attentively and with great interest to Casement's proposals for German assistance to Ireland to gain her independence. He agreed with the suggestion of recruiting a brigade of Irishmen from those captured and now in prison camps and on leaving he wished Casement ' all success in his aims and projects.' At the Foreign Office Casement continued his discussions with Count von Wedel.

If any possible doubt should exist on the score of Casement's position and authority in negotiating this help from Germany on behalf of the Irish, the following letter should remove that doubt:

' New York, Nov. 12, 1915.

' Sir Roger Casement, in a letter to Mr. Joseph McGarrity, written on August 15, and received November 6, through the courtesy of the German Foreign Office, complains that Mr. George Freeman, in a letter to Dr. Schiemann, dated July 12, makes the assertion that " everyone regrets that Casement was sent over." Dr. Schiemann had sent Mr. Freeman's letter to Sir Roger Casement.

' On account of the high standing of Dr. Schiemann and the possibility that Mr. Freeman's statement may be accepted by the German Government as representing the views of the Irish Nationalist leaders in America who sent Sir Roger Casement to Germany, and of whom he is still the duly accredited Envoy, my colleagues have requested me to give an emphatic and categorical contradiction to the said statement. We have the fullest confidence in Sir Roger Casement; there has never been since he went to Germany any lack of confidence in him on our part, and we fully appreciate and feel grateful for the splendid service he has rendered to the Irish Cause by obtaining from the German Government a declaration of its friendship for Ireland and its recognition of Ireland's right to National Independence. We also fully appreciate the service he rendered to both Germany and Ireland by the publication of his work " Ireland, Germany and the Freedom of the Seas."

' Through the courtesy and goodwill of the German Embassy in America, we have, since the outbreak of the war, been able to keep up unrestricted communication with Sir Roger Casement, though the process is necessarily and regrettably very slow, and I have during all that time been able to hand to Captain von Papen, the Military Attaché, such communications and suggestions as we wished to reach the German Government. These were always in writing and were the only communications which represented the views of the Irish Nationalist leaders in America.

' Mr. George Freeman, whose work for Germany we fully appreciate, is not a member of our organisation, and has no authority to speak for it, or for any of its members, and his statement that " everyone regrets that Casement was sent over " has no foundation whatever.

' While Mr. Freeman has a wide acquaintance, we know our people in all parts of the United States much better than he, and we can safely say that Sir Roger Casement's work in Germany is recognised by all Irish Nationalists as of the first importance.

' We hereby certify to the German Government that Sir Roger Casement has authority to speak for and represent the Irish Revolutionary Party in Ireland and America.

' Very respectfully,

' John Devoy,

' Secretary.'

CHAPTER XVIII

ATTEMPT TO FORM AN IRISH BRIGADE

On April 16th, 1915, Joseph Plunkett, the son of Count G. N. Plunkett, arrived from Berne, Switzerland, with the latest news of the position in Ireland. He gave what assistance he could in endeavouring to form the proposed Irish Brigade but with little success. It was about then that Casement said to these Irishmen in the camps in the course of an address:

' It is idle to talk of Irish liberty if we are not men enough to fight for it ourselves. We are told sometimes that Ireland will be made free by the acts of others, that if Germany were to win the war there would be a free Ireland. If Irishmen themselves are not prepared to fight for Ireland and to risk their lives in that cause then it is idle to talk of Irish liberty, and cowardly, too. To expect

Germans or others to free our country, when we ourselves are not prepared to risk anything for it is cowardly and contemptible in the extreme.'

But it was a waste of time addressing patriotic sentiments to these and eventually with the greatest reluctance he gave up the endeavour to gain more recruits. The event proved that of the small number who offered to assist this body two of the first to join turned out to be traitors. One of them, Beverley, who accompanied Casement to Ireland gave King's evidence against him for the trial in London, which assisted the prosecuting lawyers, F. E. Smith and his friends to get a conviction. The other one, Quinlisk, who was the first to come forward and join the Brigade with pretended enthusiasm for the project was later proved to be a traitor, a dangerous spy and informer. He almost succeeded in effecting the capture of Michael Collins, the Irish leader, but being caught in an act of treachery, he was tried and shot by order of the Irish Republican Army. It would be interesting to know how much the failure of Casement's plan was due to this person in whom Casement placed so much trust that he appointed him to address the prisoners in groups of thirty at a time and then to interview those who offered to join. This scoundrel was probably in English pay at the time and he had it in his power to sabotage the whole patriotic effort of Casement.

It is unnecessary to recount the difficulties and obstacles which met Casement in his vain effort to recruit a regiment of Irishmen out of the prisoners in the Limburg and other prisoner camps. From the outset the red tape of the official Army authorities combined with the vexations, interrogations and questionings irritated and bitterly antagonised the prisoners. In addition probably subtle spy action by Britain had a deciding effect. At any rate, when Casement endeavoured to reason with them and show them how they could help their country the great majority had already decided not to co-operate.

In October, 1915, there arrived in Germany from America Captain Robert Monteith, a gallant soldier who was exiled from Ireland for his work in organising and drilling the Volunteers. He was sent by the Irish-Americans to assist Casement in his efforts to promote German military assistance in the approaching struggle for Irish independence. With his knowledge of military discipline, strategy and tactics, and his training in the use of the machine gun he was an invaluable acquisition to Casement's campaign in the recruitment and training of a military unit for active service in Ireland.

Taking command of the small force in November, Monteith lost no time in putting the men in training and he soon formed them into a cohesive and well disciplined unit thoroughly well instructed in machine gun practice. Monteith, a man of vision, saw the supreme importance of having a small highly trained body of skilled machine-gunners available who would cover the landing of arms and equipment in Ireland on the appointed day.

CHAPTER XIX

MUNICH. SECRET LETTERS TO THE GERMAN GENERAL STAFF

In January, 1916, seeing little prospect of any further success for his venture and suffering from serious deterioration in his health, Casement, on medical advice, spent a few weeks in a nursing home in Munich.

In mid-February, on the urgent request of Mr. T. St. John Gaffney, late U.S. Consul at Munich, who had been one of the organisers with Judge Cohalan and Mr. Jeremiah O'Leary of the Irish Race Convention and who was at this time the official representative in Europe of the Friends of Irish Freedom, Casement, although still very ill, came up to Berlin where he spent two weeks in discussions, consultations and interviews. Casement wrote:

' In February, 1916, my friend Gaffney dragged me from my hospital in Munich to see a man in Berlin who, it was thought, could smuggle me over to U.S.A. I withhold the name. The man went to arrange the way and was never seen again. We believed in Berlin the English collared him and took him off the ship at Kirkwall.'

Early in March, 1916, he returned with Mr. Gaffney to Munich and there he wrote a very important article on Ireland which was published in the Münchener Zeitung.

British Legation,
Christiania.
Norway.

On behalf of the British
Government I promised that if,
through information given by
Adler Christensen, Sir Roger
Casement be captured either with
or without his companions, the
said Adler Christensen is to receive
from the British Government
the sum of £5000 to be paid
as he may desire.

Adler Christensen is also to
enjoy personal immunity & to
be given a passage to the
United States should he desire it.

— M. del. Findlay
H. B. M. Minister

Facsimile of Findlay's letter which he handed to Christensen when he demanded
a written guarantee of money and protection. Christensen gave the letter to
Casement. (*see page* 73)

15/5/82

Yours very truly
Chas S Parnell

Dear Sir,

I am not surprised at your friends
anger but he and you should know
that to denounce the murders was
the only course open to us. To do
that promptly was plainly ~~the way by~~
~~some~~ our best policy.

But you can tell him and all
others concerned that though I regret
the accident of Lord F Cavendish's
death I cannot refuse to admit
that Burke got no more than his
deserts

You are at liberty to show
him, and others whom you can trust
also, but let not my address be
known. He can write to Hmse of Commons

Facsimile of one of the forged letters aimed to incriminate Parnell in the Phœnix
Park murders ; published in *The Times* 18th April, 1887. The forgery was proved
at the trial of Parnell.

At this period two very urgent and secret letters arrived in Berlin from New York via Rotterdam for the German Government which were passed on to the German General Staff. The first reads:

' J.No. 109/16.

New York, February 10, 1916.

' MOST SECRET.

" Extract from report of Confidential Agent, John Devoy, on the position in Ireland, which has been delivered to the Imperial Embassy for telegraphic transmission:

" Unanimous opinion that action cannot be postponed much longer. Delay disadvantageous to us. We can now put up an effective fight. Our enemies cannot allow us much more time. The arrest of our leaders would hamper us severely. Initiative on our part is necessary. The Irish regiments which are in sympathy with us are being gradually replaced by English regiments.

" We have therefore decided to begin action on Easter Saturday. Unless entirely new circumstances arise we must have your arms and munitions in Limerick between Good Friday and Easter Saturday. We expect German help immediately after beginning action. We might be compelled to begin earlier.

" The Confidential Agent will advise (the Irish) if at all possible to wait, and will point out the difficulties in the way of (our) giving help, but nevertheless believes that circumstances make delay impossible. The Committee here will come to a decision independently.

" War Intelligence Centre,
" SKAL." '

A week later a letter was sent from the German Ambassador in America, Count Bernstorff, addressed to the German Government. This reads:

' The Irish leader, John Devoy, informs me that rising is to begin in Ireland on Easter Saturday. Please send arms to (arrive at) Limerick, West Coast of Ireland, between Good Friday and Easter Saturday.

' To put it off longer is impossible. Let me know if help may be expected from Germany.

' Bernstorff.'

While Casement was invalided at Munich, Captain Monteith was sent for by the German General Staff when the question about the quantity of arms to be sent to Ireland was discussed, and Monteith was despatched at once to Munich with certain proposals and suggestions to be put before Casement for his advice. At a result Casement prepared a memorandum which he gave to Monteith to present to the German General Staff.

In this document he emphasised the supreme importance of sending exact information to the Irish Volunteers as to the time, the date, and the landing place of the shipment of arms. He suggested that a submarine would be the best means of taking this information to Ireland and he volunteered to go on this mission himself if necessity arose. At the same time John Devoy and the Irish Revolutionary Committee in America should be given accurate information on these moves.

A few days later Casement left the nursing home in Munich for Berlin where he was confined to bed for some days in his hotel. When he was able to go out he worked ceaselessly making frequent visits to the German General Staff, the War Office, the Admiralty and at the German Foreign Office. Casement's manuscript reads:

' I returned to my hospital in Munich and then on the 7th March 1916, came the sudden news of the gun-running attempt to be made in April. When I got to Berlin on the 16th March, I went straight to the General Staff and there saw the letter asking for 100,000 rifles, cannon and officers to be in Ireland by Easter Sunday. The letter was dated 16th February, 1915 (sic) from New York.

' The letter stated that a rising was fixed for that date, guns or no guns, and begged for help. The General Staff said: " We have nothing to do with this. It is your friends, the Irish at home and in America, who are doing it. It is their plan, not ours. All we are doing is giving them the arms they ask for and giving them a chance to fight . . . ." '

At one of these meetings after prolonged and careful study of an Admiralty chart of the Kerry coast, agreement was reached to send a ship to Fenit Pier in Tralee Bay with a cargo of 20,000 rifles and 1,000,000 rounds of ammunition. The ship would arrive between the 20th and the 23rd April. On April 8th Captain Heydell brought him news that the German Admiralty had agreed to his proposition and that they were placing a submarine at his disposal to take him to Ireland.

Casement developed a great regard and respect for Germany and the German people whom he referred to as:

' The stern, self-contained, self-sustaining German people.'

In a plea for justice for Germany, he wrote:

' If there be a God of Righteousness who keepeth the nations in his care, then assuredly must Germany prevail in the end against the island-realm, with its subject, gold-bought " Allies," the horrid systems of imperial exploitation of weaker peoples . . . . the cause of European freedom demands the ultimate triumph of Germany over the bitter foe of European unity and freedom . . . . Germany may go down today—will go down, I fear, today—before the piebald hordes England has called up against her with her stolen gold— but, rest assured of it, Germany will arise again, with growth and vigour in her blood and a purity of aim and soul . . . . And I shall say if I am dying to-morrow: " God save Germany " even as I shall say " God save Ireland." '

CHAPTER XX

IRISH REVOLUTIONARY COMMITTEE'S URGENT
MESSAGE

On April 6th Count Georg von Wedel of the Foreign Office sent to Casement a letter from the agent in Berne of the Irish Revolutionary Committee, Joseph Plunkett, which reads as follows:

' Berne, 5th April, 1916.
' Ashling.

' Dear Roger Casement,

' I am sent here as delegate by the President and Supreme Council of the Irish Volunteers and through the courtesy of his Excellency the German Ambassador am enabled to give you this urgent message from Ireland:

" 1. The rising is fixed for the evening of next Easter Sunday.

" 2. The large consignment of arms to be brought into Tralee Bay must arrive there not later than the dawn of Easter Monday.

" 3. German officers will be necessary for the Volunteer forces. This imperative.

" 4. A German submarine will be required in Dublin harbour."

' The time is very short, but is necessarily so, for we must act of our own choice, and delays are dangerous.

' Yours very sincerely,
' A Friend of James Malcolm.
(*i.e.* Joseph Plunkett).'

Casement's manuscript reads:—

' Count Wedel was a sincere friend of mine as well as being the official in charge of the particular department of the Foreign Office that had dealt with the Irish affair. I had not seen him since I fell ill. His letter to me said that one " Ponsonby Stalleys," " a British spy," was believed to be coming from America pretending to be an Irishman, and warning me. My answer repeats his sentence and names Stalleys and then goes on to point out that it was not of much matter since I was going to the " homeland " of British spies in a day or two . . . . I wrote a second letter to Wedel pointing out that the ship must go at all costs, and I with her and Monteith—but no one else.

' The Foreign Office replied to me and did all they could to help me. The matter did not lie in their hands, but in the hands of the General Staff, and I found out it was sanctioned by Falkenhayn, the Chief of the Staff (then with the Emperor at headquarters) . . . . There was no way out that gave any hope—the least dark and dreadful path was to go myself to Ireland and leave the result to Providence, or Fate, or Destiny. That I did—and the result is what I anticipated. Providence met me at Curraghane fort in the shape of two R.I.C.'s who handed me over to John Bull. . . . '

In regard to the use of the word ' Ashling,' a corruption of the Irish word ' aisling ' which denotes a particular type of Irish poetry,

the following message from the German Embassy, Washington, to
the German Foreign Office, Berlin, dated 21st March, 1916,
gives an explanation:

' In case the trawlers are fitted with wireless they are to make the
following signals in the Limerick expedition: As a sign that ships
are coming, FINN. As a sign that something untoward has
occurred, BRAN. If the trawler is not fitted with wireless then send
wireless from Germany. There are numerous private receiving stations in Ireland. BRAN sent from Germany is to have the meaning
that something has gone wrong. The addition of a date means the
date to which the expedition has been postponed. FINN means
that the cargo has left at the right time. If submarines proceed into
Dublin Bay in connection with the landing of war material or
officers, then the signal is ASHLING. If only submarines come, no
signal is necessary. They are then to go straight up to the Pigeon-
house, where they can proceed in and out at any time. No nets have
been set.' And the following passage from a message dated March
13th:

' In case a submarine should come into Dublin Bay in connection
with landing of anything, either material or officers, the signals
" Ashling " would ensure immediate recognition.' In a memorandum (unpublished) dated 24th August, 1915, at Munich, and sent to
Captain Nadolny, Casement wrote:

' M. P. left a password to introduce any possible messenger from
Ireland—" Ashling." '

At an arranged point, namely Inishtooskert, to the North West
of the Seven Hags Rocks the arms and ship were to arrive after dark;
she was to show for some time two green lights. That the meeting
point and the signals were as stated is established by the following
entry in Casement's letters:

' March 4, 1916, 2009.

' No. 572 of 1st March.

' In reply to telegram 675 of 17th February.

' Between 20th and 23rd April, in the evening, two or three steam-
trawlers could land 20,000 rifles and 10 machine-guns, with ammunition and explosives at Fenit Pier in Tralee Bay.

' Irish pilot-boat to await the trawlers at dusk, due north of the
island of Inishtooskert, at the entrance of Tralee Bay, and show two

green lights close to each other at short intervals. Please wire whether
the necessary arrangements in Ireland can be made secretly through
Devoy. Success can only be assured by the most vigorous efforts.'

Another proof is a despatch from the German Embassy in
Washington to the Foreign Office in Berlin. It reads: —

' It (the landing) was to be at Tralee Bay, at Fenit Pier. The
steamer with the rifles would come to " Inishtooskert ' (N.W. of
the " Seven Hags " Rocks, north of Royal Point), between April
20 and 23. The Irish were to have a pilot there to bring her to Fenit.
The pilot boat was to show two green lights (after dark, only for a
short time). This information, they said, had been cabled over to
John Devoy, and his reply " all right," dated March 14, was shown
to me.'

CHAPTER XXI

THE ARMS SHIP AT FENIT PIER

The arms ship which was named the ' Aud ' arrived at Fenit
pier late in the evening of the 20th and the captain, Karl Spindler,
has stated in his book that he gave the agreed signals, namely by
displaying two green lights intermittently. After cruising aimlessly
about for some hours at great risk to his crew he was obliged to
steer out again to sea in order to get out of view of the land in the
approaching daylight. Next evening at about 6 p.m. near the
mouth of Tralee Bay the ship was stopped by an English naval
patrol vessel and captured after the firing of some shots across her
bows.

The German captain, however, rather than allow his vessel to fall
into the hands of the enemy and having previously arranged the
necessary explosives for such an event abandoned his ship and blew
her up. She sank in a very short time with her cargo of 20,000
rifles and 1,000,000 rounds of ammunition. The captain and crew
were taken prisoners and jailed in England. Why the Irish Volunteers did not show up has never been fully explained. The most
probable explanations may be: imperfect organisation; confusion
of time and dates; and probably poor visibility of the signal lights
on the ship (they were only paraffin lamps); and no wireless in-
stallation on the ship.

Captain Karl Spindler's account reads:

' Thursday, 20th April; 4.15 p.m. We were at the very spot—
exactly a mile north-west of Inishtooskert, a long, low-lying island
which was entirely uninhabited. . . . .

' Now for it! With eager expectation we awaited the men who
were to meet us here, and on whom it now depended whether our
mission should be carried to a successful issue. For the last half
hour we had had hanging from our bridge-rail the signal agreed
upon with Casement. . . . . I got out my secret orders and read
them through once more. There could be no doubt; I was at the
right spot, and exactly at the right time. But where were the Irish?
My orders were: " If, after half an hour's wait, none of the afore-
said vessels or persons are at the rendezvous, and there does not
appear to be any possibility of communicating with them, you are
to use your own judgment as to whether to proceed in or to turn
back." . . . . I decided to explore the inner part of the bay. At
half-speed I headed for the shore between Fenit and Kerry
Head. . . . . We could now see the first signs of Fenit, a little pier
with a lighthouse. . . . .

' The pier was now so close to us that with the glasses we could
make out every object upon it; so, of course, everything on board
could be equally clearly seen, if anyone was watching us. After we
had steamed all round the upper part of the bay, however, all hope
of this kind had to be abandoned. Though we showed our signals
more and more boldly as time went on, no one took the slightest
notice of us.

' For two solid hours we had been cruising about in the bay
. . . . . when night fell instead of flags we now used a green light,
which we showed at short intervals both towards land and sea.
Hour after hour passed and nothing happened. . . . . As midnight
drew near, it became noticeably brighter—no wonder, for towards
one o'clock the moon would rise. I once more approached the pier,
this time within six hundred yards, and at the risk of discovery
showed my green light once again. Then when this last attempt
proved fruitless, I steamed slowly back to the rendezvous off
Inishtooskert. . . . . Hour after hour passed, and as morning
approached my hope that the Irish would manage to communicate
with us during the night gradually faded away. When at last day
dawned, I gave up the game for lost.'

Casement put it down to imperfect organisation. His aims are in his own handwriting among his papers where he says his plan was to land the guns and arm the volunteers—to endeavour to postpone the Rebellion and if this were not possible that he would join and fight with them. His last words to the German authorities when leaving Wilhelmshaven on the submarine were:

' Stand by to send another ship, if we cable or send a wireless message.'

CHAPTER XXII

CASEMENT LANDS FROM SUBMARINE U-19

On April 21st at 3 a.m., while the ' Aud ' was still near by in Tralee Bay, there landed from the German submarine the U-19 on the lonely shore of Kerry at Banna Strand, Casement, Monteith and Bailey (Beverley); the latter chosen by Monteith at short notice on account of his special proficiency in the use of the machine-gun. They had left Wilhelmshaven in the submarine U-20 but when this vessel developed some slight mechanical trouble they were transferred at Heligoland to the U-19. Again there was nobody to meet them and so, leaving Casement concealed in an ancient earth mound known locally as McKenna's rath or " fort," the two others set out on foot for Tralee which they reached at 7.0 o'clock in the morning. Here they were treated with the greatest suspicion, and it took all Monteith's suavity and address to obtain some food and an opportunity of drying his sodden clothing. It was many hours before he succeeded in making contact with the Volunteer leaders. During these precious hours while he was in the greatest anxiety to return and rescue his chief, he received the news that Casement had been captured. Casement's manuscript reads:

'The whole disaster of my capture really came about through my being so ill. For three months before sailing I had been mostly in the doctor's hands . . . . I was wholly unfit physically for the strain but there was no one else. I could not send poor Monteith —or two or three soldiers—*no one could go but myself.* That was obvious—and the misery of it was that the only man needed was quite unfit at the time. . . . I was face to face with the journey alone. Monteith had said from the first moment however he would never let me go alone. Sometimes he urged me to stop the whole shipment—to stop the steamer. I said " *that can't be done*. Don't you see—these men in Ireland say they will rise on the 23rd April *in any case, guns or no guns, steamer or no steamer;* if I do anything to stop the ship I shall betray them and leave them in the lurch. No—the ship must go and I must go—there is nothing else for it." So thus it was settled and then at the last moment Monteith asked me to allow him to bring Bailey. He said Bailey would break his heart if left behind—I agreed but with a doubt as to the wisdom. Bailey was told everything all right on the night before we sailed as I have written elsewhere, and we finally got off in the submarine on the 12th April—about 9 a.m. from Wilhelmshaven. " U.20 " was this, the chosen submarine. Had she not broken down I think all would have been well—as her captain would have landed us *dry* at Tawin, County Galway, and with the boat taken back to the submarine no trace would have shown and I could have got to Dublin probably on the 18th or 19th April. That was my plan—and if I had got there the whole history of Ireland would have been different.

' The swamping of the boat on the sands of Tralee Bay, her abandonment in our haste to get clear and then my fatal staying in the old fort at Curraghane instead of going on with Monteith and Bailey to Tralee. Had I done so then I should probably have got to Dublin next day, Saturday, 22nd April—because it was by my capture and getting the *code* on me they *smelt* the steamer and seized her—without me and the code they found on me they would merely have been hunting for " 3 Germans "; they would have known this—i.e. Germans—from the pistols, bags, etc. —the pistols, mausers and the " daggers " (army knives).

' My reasons for staying on in the fort rather than going on were good—I thought so—and Monteith, too. But as fate wills—they proved fatal, and I was found there. I had just time to hide the letters I speak of, the Treaty, etc., in the rabbit hole whose position is indicated elsewhere. I saw the policeman coming. I was just going to destroy the *code* because I had decided on another way of communicating with Germany and had tried with my " firebox " (no matches—all wet), and so I was tearing the code in two. I intended tearing it in tiny bits—another three or four minutes and it would have been done—when the policeman came. I saw him coming, crumpled the code up and hurried to hide the letters.

I had intended to start from the fort across country towards Tralee and was on the point of doing this, intending to take only the letters, Treaty, etc., with me and to tear up the code into tiny fragments and bury them when the policeman came and the sergeant behind him.

' Burying the bags and pistols down by the shore was Monteith and Bailey's doing. It was as much as I could do to carry the large saturated " ulster " coat and the bag I had. They urged the burying of the pistols, cartridges, etc., etc., and keeping only the coats—and I agreed. It should have been the other way. To have thrown away the coats would not have alarmed the finders so much—as they had no German names on them and one (mine) was an old Irish " ulster." If we had made off with the bags and pistols—then the only things would have been the boat (*and* one dagger found in her! —of German make) and the three unidentifiable coats. One reason for burying the pistols, etc., was due to a decision of mine. I said before landing that we must decide quickly what we should do in the event of a coastguard patrol or R.I.C. patrol catching us on the shore. *They* would not shoot first, because they would not know who we were and would be thinking only of finding out what we were doing landing at 3 a.m. and of arresting us. Whereas *we* should know who they were and all the danger this appearance meant. So it was clear we could shoot them easily with our mauser pistols before they'd have a chance, and so get off. But I said : " Well, I am not going to shoot like that—the men would be practically un-armed men doing their duty—and it would be murder, and I am not going to have my first act on landing again in Ireland an act of murder." The two others agreed to abide by my wish—and they got a piece of tarred rope from the captain of the submarine with which we hoped to be able to tie up any *man,* or possibly two men, who might interrogate us on landing. (Both M. and B. are good shots and could have easily accounted for the coast guard or police with first shots—the Mauser pistols had 11 cartridges each.)

' Once we had buried the things in the sand, we hurried off until we got to the old fort at 5 a.m. It was getting broad daylight, and I said : " Let us hide the coats here " (they weighed a ton each!), and then, seeing it was a good hiding-place, *I stayed.* (Do you know what moved me? I saw *two magpies* as I ran into the ditch round the fort, and I said to Monteith the old rhyme, and said " Here's good luck!" He said : " Yes, Sir Roger, stay here and wait.") They were to be back or send for me by 8 a.m. " at latest." Those were poor Monteith's last words. I waited—6 a.m., 7 a.m., 8 a.m., 8.30, 9 a.m.—and then began to get alarmed. I waited too long. Had I gone out even at 10 a.m. I would have met the motor-car coming for me with *Stack and Collins.*

' I fear they have caught him now (I saw two days ago of an arrest at Tralee, and it sounded like him) and they will, if so, put him up, too, for trial. Can they? I mean for trial with B. and me? They will surely play on Monteith and tell him all the lies they can lay their tongues to, to entrap him with some " confession " or " statement."

' Monteith is very staunch, brave and faithful—the most faithful friend man ever had. He came knowing he was going to death just to shield and help me.'

CHAPTER XXIII

THE TOWER OF LONDON. 'THIRD DEGREE'
AND TORTURE

At 1.30 in the afternoon he was taken to Ardfert Barracks by two policemen. Here he remained all that day. The next day, April 22nd, he was put on the train with *one* policeman as an escort for the town of Tralee which was reached uneventfully.

While waiting for the train to Dublin, Casement was kept at Tralee R.I.C. barracks and was then sent off on the train to Dublin with a long halt at Killarney, escorted by *one* R.I.C. The journey was continued from Dublin to London where he was taken to Scotland Yard and later the same day, Easter Sunday, 23rd April, he was lodged in Brixton Jail. The following day, 24th April, he was removed to the Tower of London, that fortress in which in the past many Irish chieftains and leaders were done to death or left to rot in its dungeons. Casement's manuscript reads:

' Easter Sunday at Scotland Yard. On Monday 24th April brought again to Scotland Yard. On Tuesday morning 25th taken again to Scotland Yard.

' Basil Thompson falsely told me that both Bailey and Monteith were captured and had made " full statement ". This was to surprise me into admitting their names but I said only, " They were brave and faithful gentlemen."

' At the Tower on the morning 28th April the adjutant said he had received orders to take all papers, writing material, etc., from me and to refuse to allow me to communicate with anyone. On Wednesday, 26th April, two soldiers had been put into the room, never to leave me and to look at me all the time—and the sentry outside looking through the single pane. Three men with eyes never off me night and day—changed every hour—and electric light full on at night—so that sleep became impossible—and thought became a page of Hell.

' From that on, 28th April until Gavan Duffy called (9th May), I was in despair. I was " incommunicado ", a prey to the most distracting thoughts a man ever endured and of sorrow for what I knew was happening to Ireland. One of the young Welsh corporals guarding me had told me in whispers on Monday 1st May that many of the rebels had been shot. He mentioned Connolly, Pearse, and Clarke and " Donaty ".

' A corporal King, of Greenwich; I want his name kept—I gave him a message to M. F. Doyle in America! Strange. This was on Monday, 1st May, and I was then *very* ill and thought I was dying. He was very sympathetic; the only ray of human sympathy and kindness I got through all that awful time and I'll never forget him.

' Finally came Gavan Duffy on the 9th May. In the interval from 1st May to 4th May I was threatened by the regimental doctor with forcible feeding. I had given up eating altogether. I promised I'd try and did eat something but I scarcely ate anything till I got to Bow Street. That was the first day I ate two ounces of meat. In the Tower I had gone several days with no food at all and then only bites of bread. . . . The " interrogatory " at Scotland Yard was carried out by Basil Thompson.

' The Crown may have arrested Monteith. . . . I want him at all costs to get off the harsher punishment.

' They know all about Devoy and the Clan from their legion of spies in America. Captain Hall of the Naval Intelligence Division told me at Scotland Yard they had " got von Igell's papers ". Von Igell was a German attaché who succeeded von Papen, the dismissed military attaché, in December, 1915. Von Igell's office was raided by the U. S. law officers and all the documents seized. Captain Hall said to me that in these papers were proofs of *more than one armed ship* to be sent to Ireland. I know of course quite well that the Clan were in close touch with von Papen after I left U.S. in October, 1914. Up to that—no. I met him first and I met Bernstorff.

'The Clan-na-Gael argument was as follows: "The Irish Volunteers are going to fight to resist disarmament—they will do so whether we help or not—our duty is to help if we can."'

Captain Monteith, although hunted for months, managed to escape to America. Bailey was captured in Tralee the day after he arrived there.

It is curious that the notion has been spread that Casement came to Ireland to stop the Easter Rebellion. He did nothing of the sort. Through his instrumentality a shipload of arms and ammunition was sent from Germany to the shores of Ireland for one purpose, and one purpose only, namely to arm the Irish Volunteers for the now inevitable Easter Rebellion. Many machine guns, 20,000 rifles and 1,000,000 rounds of ammunition lay in this ship for 24 hours, and for some unexplained reason no effort was made by the Irish to take them ashore.

The following letter, the last of Casement's as a free man, written on board the submarine U-19, an hour or two before landing from the submarine, shows clearly that he meant to fight, and that the Volunteers were to fight. In this he says that he 'was meeting friends in Tralee in the morning.' He had written to Graf von Haugwitz for more arms to be sent to him by submarine, hoping that local forces would defend themselves and hold out until the further supply of arms arrived. He asked also in his letter for a further supply of machine-guns and some men to use them.

He was so hopeful of success in the South West of Ireland that he aimed at keeping Tralee Bay open as a port of call for submarines bringing 'further guns, etc.' He assures the submarine commanders 'that they would have friends in all the fishing-boats in the shore waters there.'

This can only have one meaning, namely that Casement came to fight against English rule.

In this same letter he states that he plans to secure Limerick and the Shannon so that the submarines carrying further help could reach that city directly.

This authentic letter written by Casement on board the submarine at 6.0 p.m. on the very same evening that he came ashore on Banna

Strand, is full and complete evidence of his plans to take part in the rebellion. Here is the complete letter addressed to Captain Heydell, of the German Admiralty, and handed to the Submarine Commander Oberleut Walter.

'Nearing Shannon Mouth,
'20th April, 1916.
'6 p.m.

'Dear Captain Heydell,

'A few lines to thank you and your chief for the kindly hospitality of "U-19." We were very sorry to lose "U-20" and her charming Captain and officers—but Oberleut Walter has been very kind and helpful on board this boat. I am hopeful of landing tonight in darkness, near Ardfert and meeting friends in Tralee in the morning.

'I have written Graf von Haugwitz of the Gr. Garl. Stab. about further help if possible by a submarine later on, if we can hold out.

'I think by submarine will be the only way to send up further supplies of guns, etc., after this landing, and if you hear we are holding out then any machine-guns and a few more men may be a help.

'The next few days will settle a good deal and if we succeed in the S.W. of Ireland we shall try to keep Tralee Bay as a port of call for submarines to bring us guns, etc.

'It will be our only chance of communication and if we hold that part of the country for any time your boats would be sure of friends in all the fishing-boats they might meet in the shore waters there.

'Again thanking you for your help,

'Yours sincerely,

'Roger Casement.'

'P.S. Much better than Tralee Bay would be the Shannon if we were fortunate enough to get Limerick and hold it. Then you could send submarines up the Shannon without great risk if we were in force in the city and neighbourhood.

'But the whole thing is a problem of which I can say nothing certain until I learn more on shore.

'R.C.'

Casement's prison manuscript reads: —

' I want to make it very plain that I approve of the Rising—failure and all—in one sense. As a man of " travelled mind and understanding ", I should never have sanctioned it had I been in Ireland, but since those there were bent on it, I, too (like the O'Rahilly) would certainly have gone with it. And in any case, I glory at the courage, the devotion, the willingness to die for Ireland and an ideal, that those gallant men and lads have shown. They have not beaten England, but they *have* redeemed Ireland's story.

' In any case, the blood shed was shed in a great cause, as those who died fighting saw it. They went out, a handful, against an Empire.'

Comparing the fight to the struggle for a united Italy, he wrote in prison :

' Because men remembered and told with pride and anguish the story of the uncalculating devotion of those youngsters in this hopeless struggle, there grew up, as the years went on, an unconquerable purpose in the whole nation to have their country free and united. The seed that had fallen into the ground . . . . was to bring forth fruit in its season.

' These Irish dreamers and idealists who dared to die for Ireland have done, too, for Ireland what the Roman students did for a united Italy. Out of their graves in the streets of Dublin will yet arise a nobler and a greater Ireland.

' My fate, my dreadful fate, is to be reserved only for a doom of shame—not to have been given the chance I longed for to be with them and to stand and fall with them.'

CHAPTER XXIV

CASEMENT DEFIES HIS PROSECUTORS. REQUESTS FROM PRISON CELL FOR REFERENCES AND QUOTATIONS

Letter From Brixton Prison

While in Brixton prison Casement wrote to a friend the following letters which speak for themselves:

' 3299
' Sir R. Casement,
' H. M. Prison,
' Brixton,
' E.C.
' G.N.'

Quotations, etc., etc., wanted.

' 1. Get the passage in " Ch. Lever's life in his letters ", *Blackwood,* 1906 or 1907. *London Library,* in which (in 1867 or 1868, I think) Lever writes about his lunching Garibaldi and being " put on " to it by the British Minister at Florence (Lever was Vice-Consul at Spezia) so as to " get at " Garibaldi and dissuade him from championing the cause of the Fenians on his approaching visit to England. Lever says Garibaldi was " so simple " that he was " surprised " and could not understand how the English, who were always in favour of " liberty " abroad, did not approve of it *in the case of Ireland !*

' 2. Kindly go through the *Times* of beginning of this year, say *February and March,* to find a speech by (I think) Mr. Cave, M.P. The subject of the speech was this Mr. Cave said (to show that Germany had planned the war) that when recently in France he had met Mons.? (*late a Member in the German Reichstag for Alsace*) who was now a " political refugee " in France. This ex-Member of the German Reichstag had told Mr. Cave, M.P., that when he was a Deputy in Berlin he had been one of the " Secret Session " in 1901 at which Prince Bulow had urged war credits, etc., etc.

In order to prevent the further slaughter of Dublin
citizens, and in the hope of saving the lives of our
followers now surrounded and hopelessly outnumbered, the
members of the Provisional Government present at Headquarters have agreed to an unconditional surrender, and the
commandants of the various districts in the City and Country
will order their commands to lay down arms.

P. H. Pearse

29th April 1916

3.45 p. m.

I agree to these conditions for the men only
under my own Command in the Moore
Street District and for the men in
the Stephen's Green Command.

James Connolly

April 29/16

On consultation with Commandant Ceannt
and other officers I have decided to
agree to unconditional surrender also.

Thomas MacDonagh

The surrender order to the Irish Volunteers, Easter week, 1916.

POBLACHT NA H EIREANN.

THE PROVISIONAL GOVERNMENT
OF THE
IRISH REPUBLIC
TO THE PEOPLE OF IRELAND.

IRISHMEN AND IRISHWOMEN : In the name of God and of the dead generations from which she receives her old tradition of nationhood, Ireland, through us, summons her children to her flag and strikes for her freedom.

Having organised and trained her manhood through her secret revolutionary organisation, the Irish Republican Brotherhood, and through her open military organisations, the Irish Volunteers and the Irish Citizen Army, having patiently perfected her discipline, having resolutely waited for the right moment to reveal itself, she now seizes that moment, and, supported by her exiled children in America and by gallant allies in Europe, but relying in the first on her own strength, she strikes in full confidence of victory.

We declare the right of the people of Ireland to the ownership of Ireland, and to the unfettered control of Irish destinies, to be sovereign and indefeasible. The long usurpation of that right by a foreign people and government has not extinguished the right, nor can it ever be extinguished except by the destruction of the Irish people. In every generation the Irish people have asserted their right to national freedom and sovereignty : six times during the past three hundred years they have asserted it in arms. Standing on that fundamental right and again asserting it in arms in the face of the world, we hereby proclaim the Irish Republic as a Sovereign Independent State, and we pledge our lives and the lives of our comrades-in-arms to the cause of its freedom, of its welfare, and of its exaltation among the nations.

The Irish Republic is entitled to, and hereby claims, the allegiance of every Irishman and Irishwoman. The Republic guarantees religious and civil liberty, equal rights and equal opportunities to all its citizens, and declares its resolve to pursue the happiness and prosperity of the whole nation and of all its parts, cherishing all the children of the nation equally, and oblivious of the differences carefully fostered by an alien government, which have divided a minority from the majority in the past.

Until our arms have brought the opportune moment for the establishment of a permanent National Government, representative of the whole people of Ireland and elected by the suffrages of all her men and women, the Provisional Government, hereby constituted, will administer the civil and military affairs of the Republic in trust for the people.

We place the cause of the Irish Republic under the protection of the Most High God, Whose blessing we invoke upon our arms, and we pray that no one who serves that cause will dishonour it by cowardice, inhumanity, or rapine. In this supreme hour the Irish nation must, by its valour and discipline and by the readiness of its children to sacrifice themselves for the common good, prove itself worthy of the august destiny to which it is called.

Signed on Behalf of the Provisional Government,

THOMAS J. CLARKE,

SEAN Mac DIARMADA,   THOMAS MacDONAGH,
P. H. PEARSE,   EAMONN CEANNT,
JAMES CONNOLLY.   JOSEPH PLUNKETT

Proclamation of the Irish Republic.

'The point is—this Deputy was a "traitor" in deed. He *had* taken an oath of allegiance to the Emperor—he was revealing State secrets confided to him under cover of that oath, to the enemy—and Alsace is *not* Ireland! What was the "honourable" Mr. Cave doing in the company of this traitor? Did he dine with him? Did he not recoil from contact with him? Or did he think "all's fair in love and war" and welcome the revelation of State secrets by a renegade who they served to split the Germans on?

'Once I get the actual quotation and verify it, then I'll have Mr. Cave, M.P., cited as a witness.

'3. Try and find me in the English press any references to the "Polish Legion", the "Czech Legion", the "Alsatian Corps" or any other of the numerous bodies of "traitors" and "renegades" being "seduced from their allegiance" on behalf of the immortal allies to fight against their own sovereigns. There are numerous cases in this war. For instance, the Czar of Russia (before I tried *at all!*) issued a sort of pastoral, encyclical or manifesto (in *November,* 1914) to the Italian people saying *he* was going to release and treat kindly *all Austrian prisoners of war of Italian blood* and send them as free men to Italy to fight for their "Mother Country". I presume His Imperial Majesty is quite safe in doing this, and ran no risk, but I wonder wherein the moral treachery of it falls short of mine. I did not seduce any man from his allegiance or offer him freedom. I offered him a noose! I had a cause of my own. The Czar had nothing to do with Italy. She was then, on the contrary, the formal ally of Austria, evading her obligations and false to her honour.

'Later on, about February or March this year, I read in Germany that 200 *Servian officers* were leaving France *via England* to be shipped by England to Russia to take over the command of a number of Slav soldiers who had "renounced their allegiance" to Austria and had been "induced" to fight for the cause of "the small nationalities"! Of course, very moral and right as Garibaldi said, and the English surely *would* ship those 200 Servian officers to help in this holy cause. As to the Czechs, there are said to be 12 regiments of them in the Russian service now fighting "*to free Bohemia*"—and yet Bohemia *has* her Parliament and the Czech language is spoken in it—and Ireland? Ireland has got Mr. Redmond, and Sir E. Carson, and Galloper Smith prosecuting me—and Home Rule on the Statute Book be jabers!

'There are many more instances. I very much want a few expressions of English approbation of this thing when done for " the great transcending cause ", "the very existence of humanity and civilisation itself" (*vide* Sir E. Grey and Asquith, M.P.) to put beside the same English expressions of disapprobation when an Irishman does the same thing, at every risk to his neck and skin and name, for a country that certainly has an older cause than Servia or any of the other " small nationalities " Great Britain is burning to uplift by means of "seducing" soldiers from their allegiance.

  ' G. M. Trevelyan, author of Garibaldi's *Defence of the Roman Republic* (1914), states (pp. 18 and 19) that Garibaldi *had been sent to Genoa to win over the fleet to revolution: he deliberately entered the Royal Navy with the object of corrupting it from its allegiance.*

  ' (Note that Garibaldi did much more than I did. He *entered* his monarch's service and took, I presume, an oath of allegiance with the deliberate intention of breaking it. I left mine and got rid of my pension into the bargain!) Garibaldi was " condemned to death ", a proceeding which it is difficult to blame if we consider that he was known only to the authorities as a sailor who had entered the Royal Service only to betray it. When we think that if a few turns of the dice had gone differently, the father of Victor Emmanuel would have succeeded in snuffing out the lives of Mazzini and Garibaldi at this point, we may see that history is something far more wonderful than a process of evolution which science can estimate or predict. (p. 19, Trevelyan.)

  ' There is some other book of Trevelyan's John Quinn in New York told me of in September, 1914, in which I am referred to as one of those " needed by the Empire to correct the prevailing love of wealth " or words to that effect. Could . . . find the book, or the man the author—better the man.

  ' What I want to establish is this—not that I did not commit high treason, because that, of course, I committed openly and knowingly, but that I did not act dishonourably or " treacherously ". The Crown really want to convict me not so much of the offence at law as of the mean, dastardly " betrayal of my country ". I want to show that the very thing I did has been done again and again by *far* greater men, by the noblest men in history, men whom the *English* nation are asked to honour and praise for ever. Garibaldi is a case in point. He was the " hero " of the English world, and yet he did what John Devoy and the Fenians

did in 1867, and he admired them, and Lever calls him " an un-
sophisticated peasant " for this " simplicity ". (See the Lever book
quoted.)

' Work hard for me and *for Ireland* on these lines and get *all*
the references in recent histories (and in the present war) to similar
acts of " seduction " of soldiers from their allegiance to fight for
their own country, not for the King or Government they were
recruited to fight for.

' There is also the case of the Portuguese Republic, England's
" oldest ally " and latest recruit in this war. There the Portuguese
army and navy in 1910 was seduced from its allegiance and attacked
the King (Dom Manoel) and drove him from Portugal, and the
Privy Councillors and statesmen of that King who raised his army
and navy against him are *now* the heads of the allied Power
England receives to her bosom! She does not accuse them of
treachery!

'Again Servia! And such a case! In the *Fortnightly Review* of
April, or May, 1915, I read (when in Berlin) an article by some
English writer justifying the assassination of the Archduke Franz
Ferdinand and his consort on the grounds that " assassination may
be the only refuge of oppressed peoples ". Please get the reference and writer's name. When the wretched Phœnix Park men
killed Burke they were not " patriots " or men of an " oppressed
people " but murderers. But when it suits English policy the most
dreadful crimes become deeds of praise.

' In those same *Fortnightlies,* by the way, there is another article
on the Irish Volunteers, lauding me up to the skies for trying to
unite Protestant and Catholic Volunteers in Ireland. Eoin Mac-
Neill and myself are quoted and referred to with approval. I'd
like to have the article.

' I'd like the case of William the Silent gone into, too! Was
not he deep in the confidence of Philip II, and yet a rebel at heart
and only waiting his time. Did he not too " betray his allegiance "
and plan *in secret* beforehand while ostensibly in the King's Council
to free the Dutch provinces?

' Also the English classic perhaps—" the glorious, pious and
immortal memory "! The present British Constitution is founded
on an Act of the basest treachery, and some of the proudest names
in the English peerage are derived from that Act of betraying
James II, deserting him, *calling in a foreign prince and foreign*

army to overturn the Throne. Please look up and verify the names of the leaders of the Whig Revolution of 1689 and their acts to get the Prince of Orange brought over to supplant his father-in-law.'

*   *   *

The second letter requested further quotations:

' All cases that bear on my effort to get the Irish soldiers *to fight for Ireland*. The more recent the better. Major MacBride (shot in Dublin) poor chap told me *twice* of the *offer* the Irish prisoners in the Transvaal made to him to fight for the Boers. He took the offer to the President and Executive and it was rejected by one vote, that of Wolmarans, on the ground not that it was wrong or immoral but because if the Boers accepted the offer it would make the " English Liberals their bitter enemies!" It was this story of MacBride's that first put the idea into my head of getting an Irish Brigade in Germany, and it was this story I told the men in Limburg camp in *December,* 1914, asking them this: " If Irish soldiers were prepared to renounce their allegiance to fight for the Boers how much more legitimate to fight for Ireland." Colonel Lynch may know—but then he is not to be trusted today I fear and would hesitate to stand beside me *now*.

' There are certainly innumerable cases in history—English and Continental. Lord E. Fitzgerald had been an officer in the English army and fought *against* Washington—yet he too went to France and tried to bring the French into Ireland. Washington had been an officer, too, I think. Smith O'Brien, I fancy, broke two separate oaths—that of a Member of Parliament and also of a D.L. or J.P. for Clare—was it not so?

' The cases in the present war would be the most useful for me— I mean the cases on the side of the Allies. They are certainly very numerous and England, France, Russia, etc., etc., are gladly doing all they can to get Austrian soldiers to come over. The whole charge of " treachery " and " baseness " against me is cant.

' The *act* is, of course, high treason and they may stick to that and have a perfect right to hang me on it, but they have no right to pretend that it reveals " treachery of mind ", etc., etc.

' They are really attacking me not on the legal charge at all, but on something that the law has no cognisance of—*viz.*—my opinions. What they want to assert is that I had no right to hold certain opinions and be a public servant. That is nonsense. I was employed for my actions and work and they cannot show I ever failed in that while I was a public servant. The fact that I held rebel views about

Ireland is not their business any more than if I held certain religious or atheistical views. The only thing the law has a right to assail me on is: *when* did I translate my (well known) rebel views into action. My answer is clear. Not until the war and not until I had ceased to be employed or to touch any money from the Crown. I ceased to touch my pension from 30 June, 1914, and up to that date I had committed no treasonable act, nor did I then meditate treason. I had not then sailed for America. And my going to America was not treason. But once the war broke out I had to choose. Would I seek " safety ", renounce my opinions and convictions about Ireland, or, at all cost to myself, try to carry them into effect?

' I decided on the latter course. As Mr. Birrell truly said in his evidence before the Irish Commission, " the war changed everything "—it did. It was that " world cataclysm " he had once earlier referred to as being the hope of Irish Separatists. I was always an Irish Separatist in heart and thought, and since 1905-6 in deeper feeling than before. Most Irishmen are, in a way. I was not responsible for the world cataclysm. I had again and again urged the F.O. to alter their course towards Germany and had pointed out the danger of war. I never concealed that my sympathies were for Germany or that I was a rebel at heart. Had the war not come my opinions would have remained opinions only—the war came, and the whole world was turned upside down. I saw two things: 1. That Ireland *must* be kept out of the war and that as it was purely an English assault on her trade and naval rival she should do the fighting herself. 2. That if a chance existed of getting Ireland freed, or brought into the peace terms as a European entity then it must be tried.

' In this I did only what England is asserting she will do with Slav, Czech, Pole, and all the rest. She speaks of them, falsely, as oppressed by Germany or Austria whereas in each case she cites the peoples have either autonomy or conditions of life far preferable to those prevailing in Ireland. She does not care a fig for the " small nationalities" but is using her historic cant to cover her real design— the cutting up of Germany and Austria-Hungary.

' *What I did I should do again*. It is not that troubles me. The thing that troubles me is that I *ever* was a British official—and those who knew me best knew that I was pained at the fact and desired, if I *could,* to get out of the service, years before the war. Mrs. Green knows this well. Dick Morten, too. F.J.B. The famous letter to Sir

E. Grey on my knighthood was " fulsome ". It was perfunctory. My real view of these honours was shown in the curt, rude letter I wrote Lord Lansdowne in June, 1905, when I was made a C.M.G. and in my positive refusal to be invested by King Edward. I thought I had made my view and wish so decidedly clear that no further attempt would ever be made to confer an honour on me by the F.O. They knew I did not like the C.M.G., I told them so, and they should have consulted me in 1911, before the Knighthood.

' I first knew of the Knighthood in 1911 from the paper. Dick Morten came up to my room (I was there in bed or dressing) and told me. Then came Grey's letter telling me of it. Dick Morten knew what I felt. I said, " I wish they had asked me first—I thought after my previous action in 1905 there would be no fresh attempt." Had I been asked beforehand I should have certainly refused. Once I was announced publicly as a Knight it was impossible, without giving *great offence* to King, Grey, the public, etc., etc., to refuse the honour thrust unsolicited upon me. Had I done so I should have been forced to resign my post also, and at the same time to abandon the cause of the Putumayo natives. This last weighed with me, too. So I was bound to swallow the Knighthood, and that being a necessity the terms in which I acknowledged it are really beside the question. It is, in any case, a side issue. For it neither aggravates nor condemns a man's treason what his position may be. A poor, nameless man's treason is just as lawless as a Duke's—just as punishable by law. They want much more than the legal penalty. They want to damn my character as a man first and then hang me afterwards for the breach of law. They are welcome to my life and my body, my spirit is not theirs to hang or vilify. Hence it is I want some striking instances, from their own history best, of men high in the confidence of their sovereign who have really betrayed him. But all cases help. The excellent passage (P. 193) in Sir C. Gavan Duffy's *New Ireland* that I have found here in jail is very apposite—but it deals with Ireland, and the English always regard any Irish fact as outside the realm of life or history.

' When I left Berlin a Georgian Prince, whom I met more than once, a subject of the Czar, etc., etc., was getting some thousands of Russian prisoners of war, at *Zossen Camp* where my Irish were, to go with him to the Caucasus to " re-establish the Kingdom of Georgia ". He was an enthusiast, and a Christian, too. I saw his men and many Russian officers, one of them *I saw covered with medals,* were joining him, all from the prisoners of war in Germany. If the case were the other way about, how England would laud and praise that Georgian Prince and those " devoted Russian officers and men who put patriotism and the cause of their own small, oppressed people " before honours, wealth, etc., etc., etc. We know the jargon right well. The very last time I left the General Staff in Berlin to come on my fatal journey I met him on the stairs going up to the same Department. He was going to arrange the departure of himself and his men (some 3,000) to Turkey. And I can truthfully say, here in jail today, now that the horror of the disaster, or the failure and the grim tragedy are over, that I am happier here in jail with the End in view than I was ever in freedom in Germany. There I was indeed unhappy—here I am resigned. I tried and failed—hurrying to help or save them if I could, or die with them, and *then* to fail even in that last desperate hope.'

*   *   *

Casement made his will in Brixton Prison, 14th June, 1916, in which he left all he died possessed of to his sister, Mrs. Agnes Jane Newman, 5 Convent Hill, West 130th St., New York. He knew he was being hurried to the condemned cell, for he wrote in prison : —

' The result of the trial I regard as a foregone conclusion. . . . a verdict of guilty and sentence of death, in which case I shall be transferred to some other prison, to a condemned cell—and I don't know the etiquette of condemned cells.'

He gave instructions that some of his effects were to be sent to Dr. Charles Curry, 25 Wilhelmstrasse, Berlin, and to Mr. and Mrs. T. St. John Gaffney, 7 Theatnerstrasse, Munich; the Treaty document to be sent to Mr. Joseph McGarrity, 5412 Springfield Avenue, Philadelphia; his books, clothing, etc., at W. J. Allison & Co., 9 Farrington Road, E.C. :

' These have been seized, and *burgled*. I use the word advisedly. Anything taken by Scotland Yard, I presume, can be legally re-covered. Two trunks of clothing and books at my old lodgings, 50 Ebury St., S.W., seized by Scotland Yard, to be sold and proceeds to Mrs. Newman. Books at Stephen Clarke's, An Tairne Beag, Ballycastle.

' To my cousin, Gertrude Bannister, photographs of African types, etc., which were originally to be given to Herbert Ward—not for him now as he has turned against me . . . . £47 to £50 in gold

I left at the old rath at Curraghane. *My* money and not " German gold "—if found should be handed to Douglas Hyde for the school fund (Miss Tubridy's school at Carraroe).

' There is a trunk of valuable documents with J. McGarrity, 5412 Springville Avenue, Philadelphia, Pa. " Record of Balfourism and crime " . . . . these should be preserved at all costs and some day used. The MSS. of most of my verses are with J. McGarrity.'

Chapter XXV

CAMPAIGN OF CALUMNY

Those who wish to conceal or are afraid of the truth must kill. Casement knew too much, and so to England his death was deemed a political necessity. Assassination was the obvious first choice. Another case of this kind occurred in the Near East after the Armistice when international rivalries were so intense the recently victorious Allies were almost privately at war. Two members of the British Intelligence system backed an assassin to stalk and destroy the guiding genius of New Turkey, Mustapha Kemel Pasha. But the project failed; the hired man could not get near enough to use his dagger.

Likewise in the case of Roger Casement, two members of the British Intelligence Service in Christiania under the direction of Findlay, the British Ambassador to Norway, hired Casement's servant to murder him. When this effort failed, a member of the Intelligence system was himself a shadower of Casement, and followed him on to his train with the object of murdering him. Casement, however, was on his guard, having been warned by his faithful servant, and by switching carriages evaded the would-be assassin.

The dagger having failed even with a £5,000 reward for Casement's body dead or alive, the British Government having captured him, proceeded with ' legalised ' or ' judicial ' assassination. For this purpose the chosen machinery was a clause in an ancient Act of the year 1351, *i.e.,* nearly six hundred years old! He was accused of ' giving aid to the King's enemies ', and under this Act they succeeded in having him condemned to death. But this was not enough. In a similar case, Colonel Lynch, who in the same way as Casement had organised an Irish Brigade to fight for the Boers against the English in the South African War, was condemned to death, but so much pressure was put on the British Government that the sentence was commuted to penal servitude. This would undoubtedly have happened also in Casement's case, and so the only method left by which his death could be assured—character assassination—was decided on.

In wartime the technique of underground warfare has resulted in the growth of the modern science of calumny (or propaganda) as a weapon in the armoury of belligerent nations. In this the awful power wielded by the printed word or faked photograph is used in the destruction of private judgment.

It has been said that the British are born masters of the sea but always amateurs in a war on land. However that may be, they are also patently masters of the direction and employment of secret service. Professional agents are employed for all purposes, including the secret distribution of forged documents, counterfeit reports and falsified photographs, as well as the 'removal' of opposing personalities who are considered to be dangerous.

The British headquarters at Crewe House, like that of other countries, was provided with specialists in every branch of its activities. These included the preparation of false documents, eye-witness testimony and affidavits (forged, of course), photographs (carefully 'edited') and faked photographs, false identity papers for espionage and counter-espionage, false passports, espionage counterfeits, the circulation and secret distribution of forged and counterfeit documents, the circulation of false rumours discrediting opponent leaders (character assassination). Expert penmen were employed in the preparation of these papers—so perfect were these reproductions of handwriting and signatures that they were indistinguishable from original documents and regularly passed the most expert scrutiny and investigation.

One or two instances will suffice to illustrate this. The famous Zinovieff letter, with its craftily-aimed propaganda, which was the product of the British headquarters, caused a diplomatic rupture between Great Britain and the Soviet.

Another very successful fabrication was the 'German corpse-factory' story. Counterfeit despatches in the German language were prepared in Crewe House, and later 'planted' in the pockets of dead German soldiers on the battle front. These were then 'discovered' when the bodies were removed for burial. The

'despatches' in German, together with English translations, were
published and circulated throughout the world. The 'despatches'
purported to be the text of a German Army Order issued by the
Headquarters of the 6th German Army. Sir Austen Chamberlain
guaranteed the authenticity of the document in a statement delivered
in the British House of Commons. He added: 'The text referred
to has been published in the Press and will be available to the public
through the usual channels.' The British Government circulated
photographs (faked, of course) showing the bodies of German
soldiers slain in battle being taken to the corpse factory, where they
were to be utilised for the production of glycerine from fat for use
in the manufacture of explosives. The authenticity of these forgeries
was vouched for in Parliament by Lord Robert Cecil and Lord
Curzon, Ministers and members of the Cabinet.

The London *Times* published: 'The German Army Order which
is in our possession was the daily Army Order, issued by the
Supreme Command of the 6th German Army, and it is duly super-
scribed Armee-Tages Befehl vom 21/12/1916.'

Some years later after the war was over on October 21st, 1925,
the British Military Director of Intelligence of the British Army
during the war, in a speech at the National Arts Club, New York
City, declared and boasted that he was responsible for the manufacture of the documents and the photographs and for 'planting'
the forgeries in the pockets of the slain German soldiers on the
field of battle. He announced that the 'Armee-Tages Befehl vom
21/12/1916, Army Order issued by the Supreme Command of the
6th German Army,' was a forgery prepared on the instructions of
the British Director of Propaganda in Crewe House, London.

At length, on 2nd December, 1925, the British Government confessed to having forged all the documents mentioned, and, having
provided the faked photographs and photostats, circulated them.

Sir Austen Chamberlain (who had previously in the House of
Commons vouched for the truth and authenticity of these very
documents) in the British House of Commons, 2nd December, 1925,
admitted the falsity of all the documents, and he concluded by saying: 'I trust that this false report will not again be revived.'

Perhaps if Sir Austen Chamberlain were alive to-day he would
be man enough to say the same of the Casement papers, which were
forged at the same time.

Here, among other activities of this mighty machine, the letters of

German prisoners, political enemies, and others were falsified, tracts and pamphlets were concocted to which names were forged and which presented the appearance of having been printed in Germany or elsewhere. Some idea of the efficiency of this colossal system of forging and publishing of spurious documents may be found in *The Secrets of Crewe House* (London, 1920), written by the Assistant Director of Propaganda in Enemy Countries, Sir Campbell Stuart.

Other forgeries which will come to mind are the documents and faked photographs showing Germans cutting off the hands of Belgian babies; dropping from aeroplanes candies to poison children; and the crucifying of a Canadian soldier. These were distributed broadcast, and credit must be given to Crewe House for their excellent propaganda value and for producing some of the most ingenious inventions of their kind.

The man commissioned for the Casement job could not have been better chosen. He was Basil Thompson, head of the secret political police, the man who had given Casement the 'third degree interrogatory' in Scotland Yard for hours *every day* from the 23rd April, to the 9th May, 1916. How Casement passed the nights in the dungeon of the Tower of London following each day of Thompson's 'grilling' at Scotland Yard is described in his own words in a paper he managed to get out later when in Brixton Prison:

'Easter Sunday at Scotland Yard. On Monday, 24th, brought again to Scotland Yard. On Tuesday morning, 25th, taken again to Scotland Yard. Basil Thompson falsely told me both Bailey and Monteith were captured and had made " full statement ". This was to surprise me into admitting their names, but I said only : " They were brave and faithful gentlemen . . . ."

'On Wednesday, 26th April, two soldiers had been put into the cell, never to leave me and ordered to look at me all the time— and the sentry outside looking through the single pane. Three men with eyes never off me night and day—changed every hour—and electric light *full on* at night—so that sleep became impossible— and thought became a *page of Hell*. From that on, 28th April, until Gavan Duffy called (9th May) I was in despair. I was " incommunicado ", a prey to the most distracting thoughts a man ever endured and of sorrow for what I knew was happening to Ireland. . . . In the Tower I had gone several days with no food at all, and then only bites of bread.'

Thompson then, secret service chief, and highly placed at Crewe House headquarters, was the ideal choice to prepare papers to blacken Casement's reputation and so destroy any hope of his reprieve. He was not alone an artist in the designing and preparation of materials for a good counterfeit document assailing the prisoner's character, but, as was shown later, well experienced in immoral conduct. There must have been, however, some noticeable flaws in the work, because instructions were given that the photostat copies were to be shown in part and only in the hand of the British agent entrusted with the copy, although typescript of some passages were freely circulated. Also, on the day Roger Casement was put to death telegrams were sent by Sir Edward Grey to the U.S. and elsewhere to all British consuls and agents to immediately withdraw the copies and return them at once to London. Not a single one has ever been seen since.

CHAPTER XXVI

SECRET HISTORY OF THE FORGED DIARIES

To elucidate the history of the atrocity diary which was circulated by the prosecution at the trial and which by innuendo they attempted to attribute to Roger Casement it will be necessary to refer once more to the Putumayo agent, Armando Normand, who was dismissed from his post following Casement's exposure of his evil doings there. There was no cruelty ever perpetrated by human depravity which had not been committed by this man upon the defenceless Indians. Casement said of him:—

'He is a man of whom nothing good can be said. The crimes committed by this man are innumerable, and even Peruvian white men said to me that Normand had done things that none of the others had done. . . . if anyone on the Putumayo deserves punishment this man should be made an example of.'

The name of Armando Normand looms most luridly in the ghastly picture of the Putumayo atrocities as an outstanding example of cruelty and sadistic perversion.

After visiting the stations of Occidente and Ultimo Retiro the

Commission had marched across the forest on a surprise visit to the infamous Normand's district of Matanzas.

Here witnesses confessed to having performed fearful crimes under Normand's orders. They admitted that Indian men and women had been left to starve to death in the stocks and the dead and the living were left in the stocks together until the stench of the decomposing bodies became intolerable. One witness said that Normand had an Indian chief burned alive in the presence of his wife and two children, the wife was then beheaded and the children dismembered and thrown on the fire. He saw Normand wrapping the Peruvian flag round a young woman stripped naked, then he soaked the flag in paraffin oil before setting it on fire and then shot her while the flames enveloped her body. This because the young girl refused to live with one of his assistants. The stench of the putrefying bodies around Normand's camp made life unbearable; the dogs came day after day to eat the bodies and the arms lying about on the ground.

The witness had seen twenty Indians murdered by Normand within five days at Matanzas and declared that Normand had himself killed hundreds in his six years in the district. He was constantly inventing new methods of torture and killing. Sometimes the victim was pinioned, held under the water until unconscious and then laid out on the river bank to die. Another method was to pinion the man in the stocks with his legs stretched wide apart and then kill him by beating him between the legs with a club.

Normand gloried in the corruption of boys and young men and instructed them in all his bestialities until they became murderous perverts like himself. The scourges they used for the flogging of the natives were made of strips of dried tapir hide somewhat like hippopotamus hide, " as thick as the thumb " and strong enough to cut the human body to pieces. Normand himself often gave as many as 200 strokes of this tapir hide before the native was dead. The Indian boys he kept were from 14 to 18 years of age. These he equipped with a sword—a machete—and he called his boys ' muchachos '. Witnesses saw Normand order one of his boys to catch an Indian and when he overtook him and brought him back the boy cut off the captive's head with the machete (sword). Normand stood by and ordered it. The boy then cut another Indian's head off against a tree stump. The smaller boys he called his ' cholitos ', these he also taught all his abominations and when older they became his ' muchachos '.

The first case that came to Casement's ears was of an Indian whom Normand attacked and threw on the ground. His boys overpowered the naked Indian and as he lay at their feet Normand had forced his legs open while he commanded one of his boys to batter the naked captive between the legs till he was dead. This was one of Normand's usual ways of butchering the natives.

Once as Casement is recording some special villainy of Normand which he has just uncovered, faith fails him and he lays down his pen:

' Enough, I will write no more today. I am sick of the whole thing . . . . I wonder where that Heavenly Power can be that has for so long allowed these beautiful images of Himself to be thus defaced and shamed in the name of a great association of English gentlemen.'. . . .

' The thing we find here is carrion, a pestilence, a crime . . . . a moral disease that religion and conscience and all that is upright in us should uncompromisingly condemn. . . . . All native joy died in these woods when these (Peruvian) half-castes imposed themselves upon this primitive people, and gave them the bullet, the lash, the " cepo " (stocks), the chain gang, and death by hunger, death by blows, death by twenty forms of organised murder. . . . . They are not only murdered, flogged, and chained up like wild beasts, hunted far and wide, but their dwellings are burnt, their wives raped, and their children dragged away to slavery . . . . God help the poor beings. Only He can help them.'

' It may be long,' Casement wrote concluding one of the most moving reports ever sent by an investigator, ' before a demoralisation drawing its sanction from so many centuries of indifference and oppression can be uprooted; but Christianity owns schools and missions as well as battleships and dividends. In bringing to that neglected region and to those terrorised people something of the suavity of life, the gentleness of mind, the equity of intercourse between man and man that Christianity seeks to extend, the former implements of her authority should be more potent than the latter.'

Through Casement's efforts an Irish Franciscan Mission was established in the Putumayo, of which Father Fergus Ryan of

Liverpool is the last living member. Father Ryan speaks in the highest terms of Casement and his work.

Normand had been brought up and educated in London and had lived in Paris for some years before going out to the Amazon. When Normand was a fugitive from justice Casement as a member of the Commission occupied his rooms in the station of Matanzas.

'Most of these criminals are fools,' wrote Casement. 'This man is not. He is the ablest of these scoundrels we have met yet, and far the most dangerous. This is an educated man of a sort, who has lived long in London. . . . . He probably, too, wishes to return to England some time, and he fears, perhaps, that things may go badly with him there. . . . . I got Normand's sitting-room given to me. It is pasted round with pictures from the *Graphic* . . . . There are also a lot of cocottes taken from some low-class Paris paper . . . . a certificate from the London School of Book-keepers, of 1904, given to him, and a certificate from some senior school of earlier date.'

Normand had left his notorious diary here and it was confiscated by the Commission and left in Casement's possession.

Some time afterwards Normand attempted to bribe two of his witnesses, and Casement writes:

'Normand is evidently seriously alarmed and WILL STICK AT NOTHING . . . . HE WILL BE AFRAID TO LET ME GO AWAY WITH WHAT HE KNOWS TO BE SO MUCH INCRIMINATING TESTIMONY, FEARING THE USE I MAY PUT IT TO. A man like that, with such a guilty conscience, will naturally suppose I am after him, instead of being after the miserable and criminal system he has been administering.'

In Normand's diary in addition to an account of his other enormities the descriptions of his abominable and unnatural crimes with his boys were recorded. Casement sent this diary with the other documents to the Foreign Office in London but owing to its disgusting features it had to be omitted from the official published report. Casement's manuscript translation of the diary in which Normand described and gloated over his immoral conduct is still in the possession of the Foreign Office.

The Normand diary is referred to by Denis Gwynn in his biography of Roger Casement as follows:—

'Both his (Casement's) published reports of the atrocities on the Congo and the Putumayo stated openly that he had submitted evidence too indecent to print. When he was preparing his report on the Putumayo inquiry, he brought back with him to England and to Ireland a mass of documents containing evidence against the worst offenders whom he placed on his black list, and whose immediate arrest he was vainly urging on the Foreign Office. He talked much to his more intimate friends about the evidence he had collected: and it is a curious fact that he mentioned to several of them that AMONG THE DOCUMENTS WHICH HE WAS SENDING TO THE FOREIGN OFFICE WAS A DIARY OF PRECISELY THE CHARACTER which he was afterwards accused of having kept himself. That diary was part of his official dossier concerning one of the South American agents of Arana Brothers, who had spent much of his time in Europe.'

Among the intimate friends to whom Casement talked of this South American's diary were Mr. Bulmer Hobson, late permanent official of the Revenue Department, Dublin, and Mr. P. S. O'Hegarty, late permanent Secretary of the Department of Posts and Telegraphs. What Casement mentioned to them about this criminal diary, each of them placed on record in the National Library of Ireland.

Mr. Bulmer Hobson's manuscript states:

'When Roger Casement returned to Ireland after his investigation of the conditions in the Putumayo I saw him almost daily, and we had many talks about the ill-treatment of the native population and of his hope of getting an Irish Franciscan Mission sent out as a means of checking the further exploitation of the unfortunate natives. He read me parts of his report and showed me photographs of men, women and children who had been tortured in the most brutal manner.

'Among other things he told me of a diary belonging to one of the worst scoundrels engaged in ill-treating the natives. HE HAD GOT POSSESSION OF THIS DIARY AND HAD TRANSLATED IT AND SENT IT TO THE FOREIGN OFFICE along with his report and other papers containing evidence against the (Peruvian Amazon) company and its employees.'

Mr. O'Hegarty's account reads:

'He was full of his Putumayo experiences and would speak of nothing else. I asked him about the men responsible for the business. . . . . He blamed most of all A MAN CALLED NORMAND. . . . . The point about him Casement stressed most was that HIS EUROPEAN TRAINING seemed to have made him more of a devil than any of his associates, who had no contact with Europe.

The Daily Mirror

ERTIFIED CIRCULATION LARGER THAN THAT OF ANY OTHER DAILY PICTURE PAPER

3.974   Registered at the G.P.O. as a Newspaper   WEDNESDAY, JULY 19, 1916   One Halfpenny.

GER CASEMENT'S APPEAL FAILS: "HE WAS THE KING'S LIEGE WHEREVER HE MIGHT BE."

[casement seated in the dock during the police court proceedings.]

Casement, escorted by a warder, leaving the Law Courts after his appeal had been dismissed.

[...] Sullivan, who was complimented by the Judges on his speech.

ve Judges forming the Court of Criminal Appeal yesterday dismissed Roger ment's appeal against his conviction for high treason without the realm. He was ing's liege, wherever he might be, and he might violate his allegiance in a foreign ry just as well as he might violate it in this country, said Mr. Justice Darling in dealing with the main point raised by Serjeant Sullivan, Casement's counsel, who addressed the Court for about seven hours. He argued that the statute of Edward III., under which Casement was indicted, did not purport to legislate for any territory that was outside the King's realm.

Court scenes. Roger Casement being taken to the condemned cell in Pentonville prison.

[*Courtesy of Miss Ada McNeill.*]

ROGER CASEMENT.

' He told me that THIS MAN'S PRIVATE DIARY RECORDED IN HIS OWN HAND DETAILS OF THE MOST ABOMINABLE AND UNNATURAL CRIMES. HE SAID THAT HE HAD SENT THE DIARY TO THE FOREIGN OFFICE AND HAD KEPT A COPY OF IT. I cannot clearly recollect now whether the diary went in with his report or subsequent to it, or whether it was the diary went in or the copy. But at any rate THERE IS NO DOUBT THAT THERE WAS EXTANT A COPY OF THIS DIARY IN CASEMENT'S HANDWRITING, and that this was either AT THE FOREIGN OFFICE OR AMONGST CASEMENT'S OWN PAPERS.'

With the Normand diary at his disposal, Basil Thompson when constructing the draft of the forgery had no lack of lurid and disgusting detail for his work. As the author of a diary seldom mentions his own name when writing in the first person, and as this translation of Normand's diary was in Casement's handwriting little beyond some rearrangement of the text and altering of dates and the incorporation of some matter identifying Casement was necessary to make up a document that would pass the closest scrutiny. Photographing extracts as well as distributing the photostats and typewritten copies of these extracts was just routine office procedure in Crewe House.

The handwriting required for these interpolations presented no difficulty to the expert penmen of Crewe House who had distinguished themselves by producing letters and documents in many languages so perfect in execution that detection was well-nigh impossible. The penmanship in the forged letters in the German language ' planted ' on dead German soldiers was a masterpiece and deceived even the German Government's handwriting experts.

There was, in fact, a magnificent team engaged at Crewe House and the work turned out from there was unsurpassed anywhere in the world.

As for Thompson, retributive justice would seem to have followed him.

He was dismissed in 1921. His forged copies of Russian documents and of the Russian newspaper *Pravda* were faulty. The forgery was discovered by the Russians, and was exposed later in the British House of Commons in a parliamentary debate. In consequence, he was called upon to resign on 3rd November, 1921.

In 1925 he was arrested in Hyde Park by two policemen who caught him in an act of the grossest indecency, proving him to be a moral degenerate. For this unmentionable sexual crime he was brought before the magistrates at Marlborough Street Police Court.

Evidence was given by the two policemen who caught him in the act. At the police station after arrest he gave a false name, and the constables swore that on the way there Thompson tried to bribe them to drop the case. Thompson pleaded that he had written much on and was studying sexual crime, and mentioned *Queer People*. He was found guilty by the court and the conviction was not appealed against. The inventions that his clever but depraved mind had attributed to Casement looked like a recital of his own practices and experiences taken directly from his own life. How simple he must have found it to record his own debauchery and have the result counterfeited by his penman into a colourable imitation of Roger Casement's handwriting, of which the Home Office had hundreds of specimens for many years.

After conviction by the court when his immoral life was unmasked to the public he was doubtless shunned by every respectable person and avoided by his friends.

To get away from public observation he retired to Paris where he appears to have lived in comparative obscurity. An Irishman who had been a political prisoner and whom he had threatened with death in 1917, encountered him near the Gare du Nord in Paris. He reminded Thompson that when giving him the third degree interrogatory in Scotland Yard, Thompson had said: ' You are now sitting in the chair that we had Casement in. We hanged Casement and we will hang you, too!' After this reminder, the Irishman said: 'The boot is on the other foot now, Thompson.' Thompson slunk away without giving a reply. Some time later his dead body was found (so 'tis said) in a room in Paris. The verdict at the inquest was ' suicide '.

CHAPTER XXVII

CASEMENT IS CONDEMNED TO DEATH. SPEECH FROM THE DOCK

While Casement was in prison, before, during and after the trial, the British Government, through the Ministry of Propaganda and Intelligence Service, instituted a campaign of calumny against him by spreading rumours assailing the character of the prisoner and by the secret distribution of alleged typescript copies of forged and counterfeit documents. That they were forgeries has never been denied although the name of the penman has not been disclosed. By means of press releases and the host of British agents abroad and through all the important British consulates in the U.S.A. and other countries, this flood of defamation appeared *simultaneously,* and in every case the propaganda followed the same pattern.

As for the original fabrication, although repeatedly challenged by biographers and research scholars to produce it for minute investigation, the invariable answer from the responsible minister, the Home Secretary, is a denial of any knowledge that such a document ever existed!

At the same time, both before and during the trial, the English Press took up the hue and cry and joined in the campaign of vilification. As an example, in the *Daily Graphic* on the days following Casement's first appearance in court, and while still a prisoner in the Tower of London, there appeared the following under banner headlines : —

'The Traitor in the Dock,' 'The Treachery,' 'The Route followed by the Renegade and Traitor.'

Meanwhile, the legal formalities were carried out with the greatest despatch, and Casement was hurried along to his doom. A necessary legal requirement in a trial for a capital offence is the appearance of two barristers for the defence. To comply with this regulation, and to speed up the 'trial,' Serjeant Sullivan, K.C., and Mr. T. A. Jones, a junior counsel, were assigned. The presiding judge was Rufus Isaacs, an enterprising and successful politician, a Cabinet colleague of Lloyd George with whom he had figured in the notorious Marconi scandal. For his political services he had been made Attorney-General (preceding Carson); then Lord Chief Justice and finally Viscount Reading and Viceroy of India. For his part as a politician in the betrayal, with Asquith, of the Irish Home Rule Bill, he had been frequently castigated by Casement.

The Attorney-General, F. E. Smith, ex-galloper to the General Officer Commanding the Ulster Volunteers, had his first great chance to reveal his brilliant gifts in the office to which political intrigue had advanced him. He poured his scorn and contempt on the friendless prisoner—the pension and the knighthood, the 'disloyalty '—it was easy going. The drawling voice lent pungency to the polished witticisms which won eager appreciation in a court crammed to suffocation. It was not often that English sportsmen had the opportunity to see an ' Irish traitor ' hounded to his death, with the dice loaded against him, the verdict preordained, and his character blackened by false accusations.

So little fair play was given to the prisoner that not only did the Attorney-General pass round among the jury the propaganda material concocted against him in the ' smear ' campaign, but actually handed copies to the counsel in open court. Judge Rufus Isaacs made matters simple for the jury.

' When considering your verdict,' said he, ' you will bear in mind that if *one* overt act out of the six alleged is in your judgment proved, that means a verdict of *guilty*.'

He further directed the jury to bring in a verdict of guilty against the prisoner.

' If he (Casement) knew or believed that the Irish Brigade was coming to Ireland with a view to securing the national freedom of Ireland.'

Evidence was given by a few informers and renegades. Casement was then condemned to death. Judge Rufus Isaacs put on the black cap and although a non-Christian crowned the hypocrisy of the whole trial by intoning the formula : —

' May the Lord have mercy on your soul!'

And so a gallant and noble Irishman was put to death for the ' crime ' of endeavouring ' to secure the national freedom of Ireland.' Well might Roger Casement have answered, like Robert Emmet when asked by the judge why sentence of death should not be passed upon him :—*

' I know, my lords, that form prescribes that you should ask the question. The form also presents the right of answering. This, no doubt, may be dispensed with, and so might the whole ceremony of the trial, since sentence was already pronounced at the Castle before the jury was empanelled.'

*   *   *

Casement's address to the court in the fourth day of his trial is among the greatest Irish speeches from the dock—perhaps it was the greatest of all, not only as a classical statement of the struggle for Irish freedom, but for the unfaltering courage with which he made it in a court-room thronged with enemies. Emmet and Mitchel, even the Manchester Martyrs, felt the presence of friends who understood and agreed with the principles for which they stood

---

* The full text of Emmet's famous speech is reproduced at the end of this volume.

trial. Casement had very few to speak a friendly word, and not a cheer to lend him heart at the end of one of the noblest orations in Irish history.

' I may say at once, my lord, that I protest against the jurisdiction of this court in my case on this charge,' said Rory of the Gael; ' and the argument that I am now going to read is addressed not to this court, but to my own countrymen. There is an objection, possibly not good in law, but surely good on moral grounds, against the application to me here of this old English statute, 565 years old, that seeks to deprive an Irishman today of life and honour, not for " adhering to the king's enemies ", but for adhering to his own people. When this statute was passed in 1351, what was the state of men's minds on the question of a far higher allegiance—that of a man to God and His kingdom? The law of that day did not permit a man to forsake his Church, or deny his God, save with his life. The " heretic " then had the same doom as the " traitor ". Today, a man may forswear God and His heavenly kingdom without fear or penalty—all earlier statutes having gone the way of Nero's edicts against the Christians; but that Constitutional phantom, " the King ", can still dig up from the dungeons and torture-chambers of the Dark Ages a law that takes a man's life and limb for an exercise of conscience.

' If true religion rests on love, it is equally true that loyalty rests on love. The law I am charged under has no parentage in love, and claims the allegiance of today on the ignorance and blindness of the past. I am being tried, in truth, not by my peers of the live present, but by the fears of the dead past; not by the civilisation of the twentieth century, but by the brutality of the fourteenth; not even by a statute framed in the language of the land that tries me, but framed in the language of an enemy land—so antiquated is the law that must be sought today to slay an Irishman, whose offence is that he puts Ireland first! Loyalty is a sentiment, not a law. It rests on love, not on restraint. The government of Ireland by England rests on restraint, and not on law; and, since it demands no love, it can evoke no loyalty.

' But this statute is more absurd even than it is antiquated; and if it be potent to hang even one Irishman, it is still more potent to gibbet all Englishmen. Edward III was king, not only of the realm of England, but also of the realm of France, and he *was not* king of Ireland. Yet his dead hand today may pull the noose around the

Irishman's neck, whose sovereign he was not, but it can strain no strand around the Frenchman's throat, whose sovereign he was. For centuries, the successors of Edward III claimed to be kings of France, and quartered the arms of France on their royal shield down to the Union with Ireland on January 1st, 1801. Throughout these hundreds of years, these " Kings of France " were constantly at war with their realm of France and their French subjects, who should have gone from birth to death with an obvious fear of treason before their eyes. But did they? Did the " Kings of France ", resident here at Windsor or in the Tower of London, hang, draw and quarter as a traitor every Frenchman for four hundred years who fell into their power with arms in his hands? On the contrary, they received embassies of these traitors, presents from these traitors, even knighthood itself at the hands of these traitors, feasted with them, tilted with them, fought with them—but did not assassinate them by law.

' Judicial assassination today is reserved only for one race of the king's subjects—for Irishmen, for those who cannot forget their allegiance to the realm of Ireland. The kings of England as such had no rights in Ireland up to the time of Henry VIII, save such as rested on compact and mutual obligation entered into between them and certain princes, chiefs and lords of Ireland. This form of legal right, such as it was, gave no king of England lawful power to impeach an Irishman for high treason under this statute of King Edward III of England until an Irish Act known as Poynings' Law, the tenth of Henry VII, was passed in 1494 at Drogheda, by the Parliament of the Pale in Ireland, and enacted as law *in that part of Ireland*. But if by Poynings' Law an Irishman of the Pale could be indicted for high treason under this Act, he could be indicted only in one way, and before one tribunal—by the law of the realm of Ireland, and in Ireland. The very law of Poynings, which, I believe, applies this statute of Edward III to Ireland, enacted also for the Irishman's defence " all those laws by which England claims her liberty ". And what is the fundamental charter of an Englishman's liberty? That he shall be tried by his peers. With all respect, I assert this court is to me, an Irishman, not a jury of my peers to try me in this vital issue; for it is patent to every man of conscience that I have an indefeasible right, if tried at all under this statute of high treason, to be tried in Ireland, before an Irish Court and by an Irish Jury. This court, this jury, the public opinion of this country, England, cannot but be prejudiced in vary-

ing degrees against me, most of all in time of war. I did not land in
England. I landed in Ireland. It was to Ireland I came; to Ireland
I wanted to come; and the last place I desired to land in was
England.

 ' But for the Attorney-General of England there is only England;
there is no Ireland; there is only the law of England, no right of
Ireland; the liberty of Ireland and of Irishmen is to be judged by the
power of England. Yet for me, the Irish outlaw, there is a land of
Ireland, a right of Ireland, and a charter for all Irishmen to appeal
to, in the last resort, a charter that the very statutes of England itself
cannot deprive us of—nay, more, a charter that Englishmen themselves assert as the fundamental bond of law that connects the two
kingdoms. This charge of high treason involves a moral responsibility, as the very terms of the indictment against myself recite,
inasmuch as I committed the acts I am charged with to " the evil
example of others in the like case ". What was the evil example I
set to others in the like case, and who were these others? The " evil
example " charged is that I asserted the right of my own country,
and " the others " to whom I appealed to aid my endeavour were
my own countrymen. The example was given not to Englishmen,
but to Irishmen, and " the like case " can never arise in England,
but only in Ireland. To Englishmen, I set no evil example, for I
made no appeal to them. I asked no Englishman to help me. I asked
Irishmen to fight for their rights. The " evil example " was only to
other Irishmen, who might come after me and in " like case " seek
to do as I did. How, then, since neither my example nor my appeal
was addressed to Englishmen, can I be rightly tried by them?

 ' If I did wrong in making that appeal to Irishmen to join with
me in an effort to fight for Ireland, it is by Irishmen, and by them
alone, I can be rightfully judged. From this court and its jurisdiction
I appeal to those I am alleged to have wronged and injured by my
" evil example ", and claim that they alone are competent to decide
my guilt or innocence. If they find me guilty, the statute may affix
the penalty; but the statute does not override or annul my right to
seek judgment at their hands. This is so fundamental a right, so
natural, so obvious, that it is clear the Crown were aware of it when
they brought me by force and by stealth from Ireland to this country.
It was not I who landed in England, but the Crown that dragged me
here, away from my own country, to which I had returned with a
.price upon my head; away from my own countrymen, whose loyalty

is not in doubt, and safe from the judgment of my peers, whose judgment I do not shrink from. I admit no other judgment but theirs. I accept no verdict save at their hands.

'I assert from this dock that I am being tried here, not because it is just, but because it is unjust. Place me before a jury of my countrymen, be it Protestant of Catholic, Unionist or Nationalist, Sinn Feinach or Orange, and I shall accept the verdict, and bow to the statute and all its penalties. But I shall accept no meaner finding against me than that of those whose loyalty I endangered by my example and to whom alone I made appeal. If they adjudge me guilty, then guilty I am. It is not I who am afraid of their verdict—it is the Crown. If this is not so, why fear the test? I fear it not. I demand it as my right. This is the condemnation of English rule, of English-made law, of English government in Ireland, that it dare not rest on the will of the Irish people, but exists in defiance of their will : that it is a rule derived not from right, but from conquest. But conquest, my lord, gives no title; and, if it exists over the body, it fails over the mind. It can exert no empire over men's reason and judgment and affections; and it is from this law of conquest that I appeal. I would add that the generous expressions of sympathy extended to me from many quarters, particularly from America, have touched me very much. In that country, as in my own, I am sure my motives are understood, and not misjudged—for the achievement of their liberty has been an abiding inspiration to Irishmen, and to all men elsewhere, rightly struggling to be free.

'Let me pass from myself and my own fate to a more pressing, as it is a far more urgent theme—not the fate of the individual Irishman who may have tried and failed, but the claims and the fate of the country that has not failed. Ireland has not failed. Ireland has outlived the failure of all her hopes—and she still hopes. Ireland has seen her sons—aye, and her daughters, too!—suffer from generation to generation, always for the same cause, meeting always the same fate, and always at the hands of the same power. Still, always a fresh generation has passed on to withstand the same oppression. For if English authority be omnipotent—a power, as Mr. Gladstone phrased it, that reaches to the very ends of the earth— Irish hope exceeds the dimensions of that power, excels its authority, and renews with each generation the claims of the last. The cause that begets this indomitable persistency, the faculty of preserving through centuries of misery the remembrance of lost liberty—this surely is the noblest cause ever man strove for, ever lived for, ever died for. If this be the cause I stand here today indicted for and convicted of sustaining, then I stand in a goodly company and a right noble succession.

' My counsel has referred to the Ulster Volunteer movement, and I will not touch at length upon that ground, save only to say this: that neither I nor any of the leaders of the Irish Volunteers, who were founded in Dublin in November, 1913, had any quarrel with the Ulster Volunteers as such, who were born a year earlier. Our movement was not directed against them, but against the men who misused and misdirected the courage, the sincerity and the local patriotism of the men of the north of Ireland. On the contrary, we welcomed the coming of the Ulster Volunteers, even while we deprecated the aims and intentions of those Englishmen who sought to pervert to an English party use—to the mean purposes of their own bid for place and power in England—the armed activity of simple Irishmen. We aimed at winning the Ulster Volunteers to the cause of a United Ireland. We aimed at uniting all Irishmen in a natural and national bond of cohesion based on mutual self-respect. Our hope was a natural one and, were we left to ourselves, not hard to accomplish. If external influences of disintegration would but leave us alone, we were sure that nature itself must bring us together. It was not we, the Irish Volunteers, who broke the law, but a British party. The Government had permitted the Ulster Volunteers to be armed by Englishmen, to threaten not merely an English party in its hold on office, but to threaten that party through the lives and blood of Irishmen.

' The battle was to be fought in Ireland in order that the political " outs " of today should be the " ins " of tomorrow in Great Britain. A law designed for the benefit of Ireland was to be met, not on the floor of Parliament, where the fight had indeed been won, but on the field of battle much nearer home, where the armies would be composed of Irishmen slaying each other for some English party gain; and the British Navy would be the chartered " transports " that were to bring to our shores a numerous assemblage of military and ex-military experts in the congenial and profitable business of holding down subject populations abroad. Our choice lay in submitting to foreign lawlessness or resisting it, and we did not hesitate to choose. But while the law-breakers had armed their would-be agents openly, and had been permitted to arm them openly, we were met within a few days of the founding of our movement—that aimed at a United Ireland from within—by Government action from without, directed against our obtaining any arms at all.

' The manifesto of the Irish Volunteers, promulgated at a public meeting in Dublin, November 25th, 1913, stated with certainty the aims of the organisation, as I have outlined them. If the aims set out in that manifesto were a threat to the unity of the British Empire, then so much the worse for the Empire. An Empire that can only be held together by one section of its governing population perpetually holding down and sowing dissension among a smaller but none the less governing section, must have some canker at its heart, some ruin at its root. The Government that permitted the arming of those whose leaders declared that Irish national unity was a thing that should be opposed by force of arms, within nine days of the issue of our manifesto of goodwill to Irishmen of every creed and class, took steps to nullify our efforts by prohibiting the import of all arms into Ireland as if it had been a hostile and blockaded coast. And this Proclamation of the 4th December, 1913, known as the Arms Proclamation, was itself based on an illegal interpretation of the law, as the Chief Secretary has now publicly confessed. This Proclamation was met by the loyalists of Great Britain with an act of still more lawless defiance—an act of widespread gun-running into Ulster, that was denounced by the Lord Chancellor of England as " grossly illegal and utterly unconstitutional ". How did the Irish Volunteers meet the incitements to civil war that were uttered by the party of law and order in England?

' I can answer for my own acts and speeches. While one English party was responsible for preaching a doctrine of hatred, designed to bring about civil war in Ireland, the other—and that the party in power—took no active steps to restrain a propaganda that found its advocates in the Army, Navy and Privy Council—in the Houses of Parliament and in the State Church—a propaganda the methods of whose expression were so " grossly illegal and utterly unconstitutional " that even the Lord Chancellor of England could find only words and no repressive action to apply to them. Since lawlessness sat in high places in England, and laughed at the law as at the custodians of the law, what wonder was it that Irishmen should refuse to accept the verbal protestations of an English Lord Chancellor as a sufficient safeguard for their liberties. I know not how all my colleagues on the Volunteer Committee in Dublin received the growing menace, but those with whom I was in closest co-operation redoubled, in face of all these threats from without, our efforts to unite all Irishmen from within. Our appeals were made to Protestant and Unionist as much almost as to Catholic and Nationalist Irishmen. We hoped that by the exhibition of affection and goodwill on our part towards our political opponents in Ireland, we should yet succeed in winning them from the side of an English party, whose sole interest in our country lay in its oppression in the past, and in the present in its degradation to the mean and narrow needs of their political animosities.

'It is true that they based their actions—so they averred—on " fears for the Empire " and on a very diffuse loyalty that took in all the peoples of the Empire, save only the Irish. That blessed *Empire* that bears so paradoxical resemblance to charity! For if charity begins at home, *Empire* begins in other men's homes, and both may cover a multitude of sins. I, for one, was determined that Ireland was much more to me than *Empire,* and that, if charity begins at home, so must loyalty. Since arms were so necessary to make our organisation a reality, and to give to the minds of Irishmen, menaced with the most outrageous threats, a sense of security, it was our bounden duty to get arms before all else. I decided, with this end in view, to go to America, with surely a better right to appeal to Irishmen there for help in an hour of great national trial than those envoys of *Empire* could assert for their week-end descents on Ireland, or their appeals to Germany. If, as the right honourable gentleman, the present Attorney-General, asserted in a speech at Manchester, Nationalists would neither fight for Home Rule nor pay for it, it was our duty to show him that *we* knew how to do both. Within a few weeks of my arrival in the United States, the fund that had been opened to secure arms for the Volunteers of Ireland amounted to many thousands of pounds. In every case the money subscribed, whether it came from the purse of the wealthy man or the still readier pocket of the poor man, was Irish gold.

'Then came the war!—which, as Mr. Birrell said, " upset all calculations ". It upset mine no less than Mr. Birrell's, and put an end to my peaceful effort in America. A constitutional movement in Ireland is never very far from a breach of the constitution, as the loyalists of Ulster have been so eager to show us. A constitution, to be maintained intact, must be the achievement and the pride of the people themselves, must rest on their own free will and on their own determination to maintain it, instead of being something resident in another land, whose chief representative is an armed force—armed not to protect the population, but to hold it down. We had seen the workings of " the Irish Constitution " in the refusal of the Army of Occupation at the Curragh to obey the orders of the Crown. And now that we were told the first duty of an Irishman was to enter that army, in return for a promissory note, payable after death—a scrap of paper that might or might not be redeemed—I felt, over there in America, that my first duty was to keep Irishmen at home in the only army that could safeguard our national existence. If small nationalities were to be the pawn in this game of embattled giants, I saw no reason why Ireland should shed her blood in any cause but her own, and, if that be treason beyond the seas, I am not ashamed to avow it, or to answer for it here with my life. And when we had the doctrine of Unionist loyalty at last—" Mausers and Kaisers, and any King you like ", and I have heard that at Hamburg, not far from Limburg on the Lahn—I felt that I needed no other warrant than that these words conveyed, to go forth and do likewise.

' The difference between us was that the Unionist champions chose a path which they felt would lead to the woolsack, while I went a road I knew must lead to the dock and the event proved we were both right. The difference between us was that my " treason " was based on a ruthless sincerity that forced me to attempt in time and season to carry out in action what I said in words, whereas their treason lay in verbal incitements that they knew need never be made good in their bodies. And so I am prouder to stand here today, in the traitor's dock, to answer to this impeachment, than to fill the place of my right honourable accusers.

' We have been told, have been asked to hope, that after this war Ireland will get Home Rule as a reward for the life-blood shed in a cause which, whoever else its success may benefit, can surely not benefit Ireland. And what will Home Rule be in return for what its vague promise has taken, and still hopes to take, from Ireland? It is not necessary to climb the painful stairs of Irish history —to review the long list of British promises, made only to be broken; of Irish hopes, raised only to be dashed to the ground. Home Rule, when it comes, if come it does, will find Ireland drained of all that is vital to its very existence, unless it be that unquenchable hope that we build on the graves of the dead. We are told that if Irishmen go by the thousands to die *not* for Ireland, but for Flanders, for Belgium, for a patch of sand on the deserts of Mesopotamia, or a rocky trench on the heights of Gallipoli, they were winning self-government for Ireland. But if they dare to lay down their lives on their native soil, if they dare to dream even that freedom can be won only at home by men resolved to fight for it there, then they are traitors to their country.

' But history is not so recorded in other lands. In Ireland alone, in this twentieth century, is loyalty held to be a crime. If loyalty be something less than love and more than law, then we have had enough of such loyalty for Ireland or Irishmen. Self-government is our right, a thing born in us at birth, a thing no more to be doled out to us or withheld from us by another people than the right to life itself—the right to feel the sun or smell the flowers, or love our kind. It is only from the convict these things are withheld, for crime committed and proven—and Ireland, that has wronged no man, that has injured no land, that has sought no dominion over others—Ireland is being treated today among the nations of the world as if she were a convicted criminal. If it be treason to fight against such an unnatural fate as this, then I am proud to be a rebel, and shall cling to my " rebellion " with the last drop of my blood. If there be no right of rebellion against a state of things that no savage tribe would endure without resistance, then I am sure that it is better for men to fight and die without right than to live in such a state of right as this. Where all your rights have become only an accumulated wrong, where men must beg with bated breath for leave to subsist in their own land, to think their own thoughts, to sing their own songs, to garner the fruits of their own labours, and, even while they beg, to see things inexorably withdrawn from them —then, surely, it is a braver, a saner and a truer thing to be a rebel in act and deed against such circumstances as these than tamely to accept it as the natural lot of men.'

*   *   *

Some time after the sentence of death had been passed on Casement, he was informed in the death cell by his solicitor, Mr. G. Gavan Duffy, of the slander campaign which was being carried on against him. He most vigorously protested and immediately instructed his solicitor to demand that the Home Secretary, Samuel, should produce in open court any or all of the libellous papers which he had been circulating. He challenged him to prove or with-

draw the vile slanders. Mr. Gavan Duffy at once, on behalf of his
client, officially communicated this demand and challenge to the
Home Secretary but this and further requests were ignored and
left unanswered. Frequent requests to succeeding Home Secre-
taries have also been unavailing.

It is no wonder Casement, in his prison cell, when made aware
that he was the helpless victim of an unparalleled campaign of
vilification, insinuations, whispered slander, newspaper attack, and
officially circulated libellous forgeries, wrote : —

' It is a cruel thing to die with all men misunderstanding—mis-
apprehending—and to be silent forever.'

*   *   *

In the days of chivalry, a candidate for knighthood fasted and
prayed on the eve of the ceremony. He was reminded of the blood
that he must be prepared to shed for the Christian faith, for truth
and justice. He swore to defend the right.

For Roger Casement's exposure of cruelty and injustice in the
Congo, which won the admiration of the civilised world, his
Britannic Majesty, Edward VII, made him a Commander of the
Order of St. Michael and St. George, King George V bestowed a
knighthood on him in 1911, when his heroic efforts, regardless of
health and worldly advantage, had made known the iniquities of
the Putumayo rubber planters.

On June 30th, 1916, the day after he was sentenced to death, it
was announced in the London Gazette that His Majesty the King
'had been pleased to degrade Roger David Casement from the
Order of Knights Bachelor'. It was three centuries since a knight
had been ' degraded ' in England. On the last occasion the ceremony
was carried out in Westminster Hall. This gentleman had his spurs
hacked off, his belt cut, and his sword broken over his head.

The kind of services for which knighthoods and other ' honours '
had been awarded in England in recent years are not usually
associated with chivalrous enterprise, or the redress of wrongs. Sir
F. E. Smith, the Attorney-General who prosecuted Roger Casement,
was ' galloper ' to Carson in the Ulster Volunteers. He galloped his
way to be Earl of Birkenhead and Lord High Chancellor of
England—who is ' Keeper of the King's Conscience ', and gets
£10,000 a year. In a famous address to the Oxford Union he advised
young men to keep their eyes on the ' glittering prizes ' of life.
Roger Casement sought no ' glittering prizes '.

Two letters written by the prisoner's solicitor show clearly the determination of the Government to take the life of Casement. The first letter was written to Mr. Michael Francis Doyle, an American lawyer who came to London in an endeavour to assist Casement, but was not allowed to appear. Mr. Gavan Duffy wrote on 23rd August, 1916:

'The session of the Criminal Court of Appeal held to see if there would be a further application in the Casement case on the 28th ult. was AN IMPUDENT DODGE OF MR. JUSTICE DARLING'S TO MINIMISE THE DEFENCE and has aroused widespread indignation in the Temple as well as infuriating our own counsel.'

The second letter, addressed to Mrs. Robert Lynd, showed what little faith Gavan Duffy had in the Court of Criminal Appeal. It contains the following passages:

'I fear it will not succeed in the event of criminal appeal, but I HAVE EVERY HOPE IT WILL SUCCEED IF THE ATTORNEY-GENERAL GIVES LEAVE FOR AN APPEAL TO THE HOUSE OF LORDS. THAT IS THE ONLY COURT WHERE THERE IS EVEN A TRACE OF INTELLECTUAL HONESTY LEFT IN THIS COUNTRY JUST NOW.'

Attorney-General Smith promptly and peremptorily refused the permission and by so doing denied the prisoner his legal right of appeal to the House of Lords—an appeal in which his legal advisers, one of them a professor of constitutional law (Professor J. H. Morgan), were confident of success. By this action, Smith betrayed the cause of justice and disgraced the Bar of England.

In this trial, the jury partook, naturally enough, of the general ferment, confirming them in their prejudices and inflaming their passions. Judges whose duty it was to guard them against such impressions were scandalously negligent in doing so. The Attorney-General, Smith, bigoted Orangeman and organiser of rebellion, 'manager' of the prosecution, and at that time a member of the Government which had shortly before offered £5,000 for Casement's body, dead or alive, acted with the political prejudice which, in the circumstances and in keeping with his past, might be expected.

Even according to the strained construction of the Statute of Edward III, 1351, the prisoner's action was legally *not* treason, so it is impossible not to assent to the opinion of those who have stigmatised the condemnation and execution of Casement as a most flagrant violation of law and justice.

The validity of pretences was little attended to in this instance and in war-time, in the case of a person whom the court had doomed to destruction and so, upon evidence from a few informers and renegades, was this great and excellent man condemned to die.

Lest the odious connection between that branch of the judicature, the Attorney-General's Department, and the Government should strike the reader too forcibly, it might be pointed out that in this instance Attorney-General Smith ought to be regarded as the mere tool and instrument of the Government which had appointed him.

The very recollection of this 'managed' trial—even at this distance of time, fires every honest heart with indignation.

CHAPTER XXVIII

" THIS MOST GALLANT GENTLEMAN."
PURSUING VENGEANCE BEYOND THE GRAVE

THIS MOST GALLANT GENTLEMAN

I saw that Roger Casement
Did what he had to do.
He died upon the gallows,
But that is nothing new.

Afraid they might be beaten
Before the bench of Time,
They turned a trick by forgery
And blackened his good name.

A perjurer stood ready
To prove their forgery true;
They gave it out to all the world,
And that is something new.

Come Tom and Dick, come all the troop
That cried it far and wide,
Come from the forger and his desk,
Desert the perjurer's side :

15.   . 37.

Dear Madam,

Thank you for your letter with regard to the exhumation and transference of the body of Roger Casement. You may be sure that when the matter comes before the House I will do anything I can to support your very reasonable demand.

Yours sincerely,

C. R Attlee

Miss S. MacDermott.

Letter from Mr. Clement Attlee, leader of the British Labour Party, to Miss S. MacDermott, Secretary of the Casement Repatriation Committee.
(*The House of Commons imprint has been darkened for photographic purposes.*)

[Courtesy of the National Museum of Ireland]

MEDAL, bronze. Obverse—Hangman tying halter round neck of figure representing Sir Roger Casement—Legend : *Englands Tatendrang*—in exergue : *Roger Casement*. Initials K.G. on a chain on one of arms of figure (K. Goetz, of Munich). Reverse—torture chair on which rests a book with inscription thereon *Englisch. Gesetz. um.* 1351. Spider spinning web which partially covers book and chair. Around—Edward III. Tote. Hand. Legt. Den. *Strang. Um*[8]. Irenland. In the field—3 *Aug.* 1916. Beneath chair—a skull, serpents, broken crown, rat. Diam. $2\frac{1}{8}''$.

(Both obverse and reverse inspired by Casement's speech in the dock—

"Edward III was King not only of the Realm of England but also of the Realm of France and he was *not* the King of Ireland. Yet his dead hand to-day may pull the noose around the Irishman's neck, whose Sovereign he was not, although it can strain no strand around the Frenchman's throat, whose Sovereign he was . . . The judicial assassination of to-day was reserved for one race of the King's subjects—for the Irishmen ; for those who cannot forget their allegiance to the Realm of Ireland.")

MEDAL, bronze. Obverse—Bust of Roger Casement to right ; around—*Roger Casement ;* initials *BM* to the left on field (B. H. Meyer of Pforzheim). Reverse—Two draped female figures seated on an arch which spans two countries. Both figures are manacled and clasp hands beneath a star, above which is the legend—*Irland und Deutschland.* That to left (one hand resting on harp) represents Ireland. Under the arch a shield of the emblems of both countries superimposed on a sword beneath which is the legend—*Vereint in Leiden.* To left a round tower and right *BM*. Diam. $2\frac{3}{8}''$.

Come speak your bit in public
That some amends be made
To this most gallant gentleman
That is in quicklime laid.

W. B. YEATS.

The vengeance of the British Government pursued Roger Casement beyond his death on the scaffold.

In violation of established law they rejected the legitimate request of the legal representative of the relations of the dead man that the body should be handed over to them for Christian burial. Instead, the Government illegally withheld his body and buried it in quicklime in the prison yard where it still lies.

If the English Government really had the will to prosecute Casement for ' murder,' it was open to them to do so. They knew, however, that in this charge they would fail, because Casement was no murderer. Instead, they charged him with ' treason ' and secured the death penalty. But, having done so, they should have conformed to established English law and given the body to the relatives for Christian burial as the law requires in cases of treason. As a piece of hypocrisy, this conduct must be almost without parallel. The action of the English Government in the matter can find no credit from men of sense and can only be considered as a most atrocious perversion of justice.

*   *   *

LEGAL CORRESPONDENCE

Between Mr. G. Gavan Duffy, legal adviser to Roger Casement and later President of the High Court, Dublin, and the Home Secretary, Whitehall, London, W.C., in connection with the execution of Roger Casement in Pentonville Prison, 3 August, 1916.

4 Raymond Buildings,
Gray's Inn, W.C.
2nd August, 1916.

Secretary of State for Home Affairs.

Sir :

I have the honour on behalf of Roger Casement's nearest relatives in England, the Misses and Mr. Bannister, and at his own express request, to entreat you that if his sentence is to be carried out *his body may be given to his relatives for burial in consecrated ground and outside the prison,* subject to such undertaking as to keeping the funeral private and such other restrictions as you may think it necessary to impose.

I trust that you may see your way to meeting his relatives in their deep grief by acceding to this prayer which is also the last wish of the condemned man.

May I also ask you to allow me to be present at the last moments of my friend and client.

I have the honour to be,
Sir,
Your obedient servant,
G. GAVAN DUFFY.

Home Office,
Whitehall.
2nd August, 1916.

31164B

Sir,

I am directed by the Secretary of State to say that he is unable to comply with the request made by you on behalf of certain relatives of the prisoner Roger David Casement that his body may be buried outside the prison as the law requires that it shall be buried within the walls.

I am to inform you also that the Secretary of State is unable to accede to your request that you may be present at the execution.

I am,
Sir,
Your obedient servant,
E. BLACKWELL.

G. Gavan Duffy, Esq.,
4, Raymond Buildings,
Gray's Inn, W.C.

3rd August, 1916.

The Under Secretary of State,
Home Office, S.W.

Sir,

I have the honour to acknowledge your letter of yesterday intimating that the Secretary of State is unable to allow me to be present at the execution of Roger Casement and that he is unable to allow the body to be buried outside the prison walls ' as the law requires that it shall be buried within the walls '. I beg you to let me know to what law you refer, as I venture to think there must be a misapprehension, for I am advised that *there is no such law in the case of treason* and if the Secretary of State will be good enough to reconsider the matter I feel sure that he will recognise that the King has the disposal of the body in his hands. If this be so, I hesitate to believe that His Majesty will be advised to refuse the relatives' request to have the body in order that Roger Casement may *not be buried with the indignity habitual in the case of a murderer.*

I write in great haste and beg for the favour of your reply as soon as possible.

In the meantime, I have the honour to be,

Sir,
Your obedient servant,
G. GAVAN DUFFY.

Home Office,
Whitehall.
3rd August, 1916.

311643/146.

Sir,

In reply to your letter of today's date, I am directed by the Secretary of State to refer you to Section 6 of the Capital Punishment Amendment Act, 1868, which provides that the body of every offender executed shall be buried within the walls of the prison within which judgment of death is executed on him.

I am,
Sir,
Your obedient servant,
E. BLACKWELL.

G. Gavan Duffy, Esq.,
4, Raymond Buildings,
Gray's Inn, W.C.

4th August, 1916.

To the Under Secretary of State,
Home Office,
Whitehall.

311643/146.

Sir,

I have the honour to acknowledge the receipt of your letter of yesterday that the Home Secretary takes the view that Section 6 of the Capital Punishment Amendment Act, 1868, applies to a case of execution for treason I must respectfully dissent from this view inasmuch as *that Act has always been considered to apply to cases of murder and none other,* and the principal Section of the Act (Section 2) as to carrying out the judgment of death is expressly confined to murder.

In view of the submission which I ventured to put before you in my letter of yesterday, *the relatives of Roger Casement consider that a grievous wrong has been done to them,* since it is apparent that the question of burial within the prison walls has never been considered by the Home Secretary otherwise than *in connection with a Statute which they are advised has no application.*

> I have the honour to be,
> Sir,
> Your obedient servant,
> G. GAVAN DUFFY.

While he was in Pentonville, Casement's mind often went back to his early days in Ireland when he walked on Fair Head and at Murlough Bay. He often spoke of Murlough. His last wish as he lay in prison was : —

'When they have done with me, don't let my bones lie in this dreadful place—take me back to Murlough and let me lie there.'

Casement's mortal remains still lie in Pentonville Jail despite the efforts of successive Irish Governments to have them returned to his native soil.

In the solitude of the Antrim hills, guarded on either side by the headlands, on the shore of the sea of Moyle, is Murlough. On the hillside is a little churchyard and in it is a little cross which marks the grave which will one day, please God, hold the mortal remains of the patriot. It is Ireland's memorial to Roger Casement. It was here in the peace of the Antrim Hills that this most gallant gentleman wished to sleep his long last sleep.

Chapter XXIX

THE DEATH CELL AND LAST HOURS

Memoir by Father James McCarroll

[*The manuscript from which these extracts were taken was in
Roger Casement's overcoat pocket in the condemned cell. Father
James McCarroll returned from the execution shed to the condemned
cell and there copied out the passages given here. Before he had
quite finished, he was interrupted by the sound of footsteps of the
Deputy-Governor, who then entered the cell and took away the
overcoat and the manuscript. These, then, are Casement's very last
written words. Father McCarroll has included them in this short
memoir of the last hours of the patriot which he sent to the author
with permission to publish. Father McCarroll was the prison
chaplain.*]

Though 30 years have passed, the years have not dimmed the
memory of a noble—gentle, lonely soul. It was a lonely place, the
condemned cell at Pentonville Prison. We met on the evening of the
29th June, 1916, Feast of St. Peter and St. Paul, and thus
began a friendship which I know has lasted far beyond the 3rd of
August, 1916, the day on which he went to God. We met on the
29th June, and we met daily until 3rd August, until his lonely burial
in the prison yard with all the rites and ceremonies of the Church.

I was the sole mourner at his grave, yet we were not all alone,
for around were the prayers of his friends—and the souls of noble
men who thought the same thoughts and dreamed the same dreams
as Roger Casement.

*   *   *

' My dominating thought was to keep Ireland out of the war.
England has no claim on us, in Law or Morality or Right. Ireland
should not sell her soul for any mess of Empire. If I die tomorrow
bury me in Ireland, and I shall die in the Catholic Faith, for I accept
it fully now. It tells me what my heart sought long—but I saw it in
the faces of the Irish. Now I know what it was I loved in them.
The chivalry of Christ speaking through human eyes—it is from
that source all lovable things come, for Christ was the first Knight
—and now good-bye. I write still with hope—hope that God will
be with me to the end. . . .

'And if I die, as I think is fated, tomorrow morning, I shall die with my sins forgiven and God's pardon on my soul, and I shall die with many brave and good men. . . .

'Think of the long succession of the dead who died for Ireland —and it is a great death. Oh! that I may support it bravely. If it be said I shed tears, remember they come not from cowardice but from sorrow—and brave men are not ashamed to weep sometimes.

'I hope I shall not weep, but if I do it shall be nature's tribute wrung for me—one who never hurt a human being—and whose heart was always compassionate and pitiful for the grief of others.

'The long waiting has been a cruel thing, three months and 11 days now. . . .

'It is a strange, strange fate, and now, as I stand face to face with death, I feel just as if they were going to kill a boy. For I feel like a boy—and my hands so free from blood and my heart always so compassionate and pitiful that I cannot comprehend how anyone wants to hang me. . . .

'It is they—not I—who are the traitors, filled with a lust of blood—of hatred of their fellows.

'These artificial and unnatural wars, prompted by greed of power, are the source of all misery now destroying mankind. . . . I shall still hope till the sheriff comes, and if he comes it is to pre-pare to go to God with calm and hope and leave all here with an infinite blessing breathed from a very finite heart. . . . No man in the world ever got so much undeserved friendship as I have found these last days. The great outpouring of love and goodness on me is the greatest proof of God's love for sinful men.

'God gave me into this captivity and death, and I kiss the Divine Hand that leads me to the grave. . . .

'Alas, so much of the story dies with me—the old, old story—yet, in spite of all—the truth and right lives on in the hearts of the brave and lowly. It is better that I die thus—on the scaffold——

'It is a glorious death for Ireland's sake with Allen, Larkin and O'Brien, and Robert Emmet—and the men of '98 and William Orr —all for the same cause—all in the same way. Surely it is the most glorious cause in history.

> 'Ever defeated—
> yet undefeated,
>
> 'Roger Casement.'

Mass was said in the prison chapel at 7.30 on the morning of his execution. It was at this Mass that Roger Casement received his first Holy Communion which was also his Viaticum. It was a day of great spiritual joy for him. He expressed a desire to go to the scaffold fasting so, as he said, that his God might be the last food he took on earth.

The intervening time between Mass and nine o'clock was passed in prayer. Quietly he submitted to the attentions of the executioner. With his hands bound, calmly he walked to the scaffold, repeating the words:—

'Into Thy Hands I commend my spirit.'

His last words were:—

'Lord Jesus, receive my soul.'

*   *   *

This little poem was given to me personally by him. It may remind friends to think of Roger Casement 'On the long road that will not ever end.'

> '*Think of a long road in a valley low,*
> *Think of a wanderer in the distance far*
> *Lost like a voice among the scattered hills.*
> *And when the moon is gone and ocean spills*
> *Its waters backward from the trysting bar,*
> *And in the dark furrows of the night there tills*
> *A jewelled plough, and many a falling star*
> *Moves you to prayer, then will you think of me*
> *On the long road that will not ever end?*'
>
> Roger Casement, 14-7-16.

EPILOGUE

At 9 o'clock on the morning of August 3rd, the tolling of the prison bell announced that Roger Casement was dead on the scaffold. The first toll of the bell was greeted by a loud and exultant cheer from the great English throng crowded outside the prison gate and each following stroke was also loudly cheered.

Shortly after, the following notice, signed by the sheriff and the prison governor, was posted on the prison gate: —

' We, the undersigned, hereby declare that judgment of death was this day executed on Roger David Casement in His Majesty's prison of Pentonville in our presence.'

This was the signal for a burst of applause and triumphant cheering from the English multitude.

Groups of Irish men and women were kneeling outside the prison gates in silent prayer. At the sound of the death bell these Irish groups joined together in reciting the Prayers for the Dead.

Who can read without horror the account of the savage murmur of applause and the triumphant cheers of the English crowd assembled at the prison gate when the notice was affixed that Roger Casement had been killed by their hangman, and how this horror deepens when we reflect that in that odious cry was drowned the prayers of those sorrowing Irish exiles gathered there to pay a last tribute to their countryman, martyred in the sacred cause of human liberty.

*　　　*　　　*

Thus fell Roger Casement, a name that will, it is hoped, be forever dear to every honest heart. When his memory shall cease to be the object of respect and veneration, it requires no spirit of prophecy to foretell that the spirit of liberty will be fast approaching to its final consummation.

His deportment throughout the trial and the long prison ordeal was such as might be expected from a man who knew himself to be suffering not for his crimes but for his virtues. In courage and fortitude the story of the last days of this excellent man's life fills the mind with such a mixture of tenderness and admiration that there can scarcely be any scene in history that more powerfully excites our sympathy or goes more directly to the heart.

THE GHOST OF ROGER CASEMENT

O what has made that sudden noise?
What on the threshold stands?
It never crossed the sea because
John Bull and the sea are friends;
But this is not the old sea
Nor this the old seashore.
What gave that roar of mockery,
That roar in the sea's roar?
The ghost of Roger Casement
Is beating on the door.

I poked about the village church,
And found his family tomb,
And copied out what I could read
In that religious gloom;
Found many a famous man there,
But fame and virtue rot.
Draw round, beloved and bitter men,
Draw round and raise a shout;
The ghost of Roger Casement
Is beating on the door.

W. B. YEATS.

PARNELL

Hush—let no whisper of the cruel strife,
Wherein he fell so bravely fighting, fall
Nigh these dead ears; fain would our hearts recall
Nought but proud memories of a noble life—
Of unmatched skill to lead by pathways rife
With danger and dark doubt, where slander's knife
Gleamed ever bare to wound, yet over all
He pressed triumphant on—lo, thus to fall.
Through and beyond the breach he living made
Shall Erin pass to freedom and to will,
And shape her fate: there where his limbs are laid
No harsh reproach dare penetrate the shade:
Death's angel guards the door, and o'er the sill
A mightier voice than Death's speaks 'Peace, be still!'

ROGER CASEMENT, 6th Oct., 1891.

APPENDIX

ROBERT EMMET'S SPEECH FROM THE DOCK

' My Lords,—I am asked what I have to say why sentence of death should not be pronounced on me, according to law. I have nothing to say that can alter your predetermination, nor that it will become me to say, with any view of the mitigation of that sentence which you are to pronounce, and I must abide by. But I have that to say which interests me more than life, and which you have laboured to destroy. I have much to say why my reputation should be rescued from the load of false accusation and calumny which has been cast upon it. I do not imagine that, seated where you are, your mind can be so free from prejudice as to receive the least impression from what I am going to utter. I have no hopes that I can anchor my character in the breast of a court constituted and trammelled as this is. I only wish, and that is the utmost that I expect, that your lordships may suffer it to float down your memories untainted by the foul breath of prejudice until it finds some more hospitable harbour to shelter it from the storms by which it is buffeted. Was I only to suffer death, after being adjudged guilty by your tribunal, I should bow in silence, and meet the fate that awaits me without a murmur. But the sentence of the law which delivers my body to the executioner will, through the ministry of the law, labour in its own vindication, to consign my character to obloquy; for there must be guilt somewhere : whether in the sentence of the court, or in the catastrophe, time must determine.

' A man in my situation has not only to encounter the difficulties of fortune, and the force of power over minds which it has corrupted or subjugated, but the difficulties of established prejudice. The man dies, but the memory lives. That mine may not perish, that it may live in the respect of my countrymen, I seize upon this opportunity to vindicate myself from some of the charges alleged against me. When my spirit shall be wafted to a more friendly port—when my shade shall have joined the bands of those martyred heroes who have shed their blood on the scaffold and in the field in the defence of their country and of virtue, this is my hope: I wish that my memory and name may animate those who survive me, while I look down with complacency on the destruction of that perfidious Government which upholds its domination by blasphemy of the Most High—which displays its power over man as over the beasts of the forest—which sets man upon his brother, and lifts his hand, in the name of God, against the throat of his fellow who believes or doubts a little more or a little less than the Government standard—a Government which is steeled to barbarity by the cries of the orphans and the tears of the widows it has made.'

[Here Lord Norbury interrupted Mr. Emmet, saying ' that the mean and wicked enthusiasts who felt as he did were not equal to the accomplishment of their wild designs.']

' I appeal to the immaculate God: I swear by the Throne of Heaven, before which I must shortly appear,—by the blood of the murdered patriots who have gone before me—that my conduct has been, through all this peril, and through all my purposes, governed only by the conviction which I have uttered, and by no other view than that of the emancipation of my country from the superinhuman oppression under which she has so long and too patiently travailed; and I confidently hope that, wild and chimerical as it may appear, there is still union and strength in Ireland to accomplish this noblest of enterprises. Of this I speak with confidence, of intimate knowledge, and with the consolation that appertains to that confidence. Think not, my lords, I say this for the petty gratification of giving you a transitory uneasiness. A man who never yet raised his voice to assert a lie, will not hazard his character with posterity, by asserting a falsehood on a subject so important to his country, and on an occasion like this. Yes, my lords, a man who does not wish to have his epitaph written until his country is liberated, will not leave a weapon in the power of envy, or a pretence to impeach the probity which he means to preserve, even in the grave to which tyranny consigns him.'

[Here he was again interrupted by the court.]

' Again I say, that what I have spoken was not intended for your lordship, whose situation I commiserate rather than envy,—my expressions were for my countrymen. If there is a true Irishman present, let my last words cheer him in the hour of his affliction.'

[Again he was interrupted. Lord Norbury said he did not sit there to hear treason.]

' I have always understood it to be the duty of a judge, when a prisoner has been convicted, to pronounce the sentence of the law. I have also understood that judges sometimes think it their duty to hear with patience, and to speak with humanity; to exhort the victim of the laws, and to offer, with tender benignity, their opinions of the motives by which he was actuated in the crime of which he was adjudged guilty. That a judge has thought it his duty so to have done, I have no doubt; but where is the boasted freedom of your institutions—where is the vaunted impartiality, clemency and mildness of your courts of justice if an unfortunate prisoner, whom your policy, and not justice, is about to deliver into the hands of the executioner, is not suffered to explain his motives sincerely and truly, and to vindicate the principles by which he was actuated? My lords, it may be a part of the system of angry justice to bow a man's mind by humiliation to the purposed ignominy of the scaffold; but worse to me than the purposed shame, or the scaffold's terrors, would be the shame of such foul and unfounded imputations as have been laid against me in this court. You, my lord, are a judge; I am the supposed culprit. I am a man; you are a man also. By a revolution of power we might change places, though we never could change characters. If I stand at the bar of this court, and dare not vindicate my character, what a farce is your justice! If I stand at this bar, and dare not vindicate my character, how dare you calumniate it. Does the sentence of death, which your unhallowed policy inflicts on my body, condemn my tongue to silence and my reputation to reproach? Your executioner may abridge the period of my existence; but while I exist I shall not forbear to vindicate my character and motives from your aspersions; and, as a man, to whom fame is dearer than life, I will make

the last use of that life in doing justice to that reputation which is to live
after me, and which is the only legacy I can leave to those I honour and
love, and for whom I am proud to perish. As men, my lords, we must appear
on the great day at one common tribunal; and it will then remain for the
Searcher of all hearts to show a collective universe, who was engaged in the
most virtuous actions, or swayed by the purest motives—my country's
oppressor, or——'

[Here he was interrupted, and told to listen to the sentence of the law.]

'My lords, will a dying man be denied the legal privilege of exculpating
himself in the eyes of the community from an undeserved reproach, thrown
upon him during his trial, by charging him with ambition, and attempting
to cast away for a paltry consideration the liberties of his country? Why did
your lordships insult me? or, rather, why insult justice, in demanding of me
why sentence of death should not be pronounced against me? I know, my
lords, that form prescribes that you should ask the question. The form also
presents the right of answering. This, no doubt, may be dispensed with, and
so might the whole ceremony of the trial, since sentence was already pronounced at the Castle before the jury were empanelled. Your lordships are
but the priests of the oracle, and I insist on the whole of the forms.'

[Here Mr. Emmet paused, and the court desired him to proceed.]

'I am charged with being an emissary of France. An emissary of France!
and for what end? It is alleged that I wish to sell the independence of my
country; and for what end? Was this the object of my ambition? And is this
the mode by which a tribunal of justice reconciles contradiction? No; I am
no emissary; and my ambition was to hold a place among the deliverers of my
country, not in power nor in profit, but in the glory of the achievement. Sell
my country's independence to France! and for what? Was it a change of
masters? No, but for my ambition. Oh, my country, was it personal ambition
that could influence me? Had it been the soul of my actions, could I not,
by my education and fortune, by the rank and consideration of my family,
have placed myself amongst the proudest of your oppressor. My Country was
my Idol. To it I scattered every selfish, every endearing sentiment; and for it
I now offer up myself, O God! No, my lords; I acted as an Irishman, determined on delivering my country from the yoke of a foreign and
unrelenting tyranny, and the more galling yoke of a domestic faction, which
is its joint partner and perpetrator in the patricide, from the ignominy exist-
ing with an exterior of splendour and a conscious depravity. It was the wish
of my heart to extricate my country from this doubly riveted despotism—I
wished to place her independence beyond the reach of any power on earth.
I wished to exalt her to that proud station in the world.

'Connection with France was, indeed, intended, but only as far as mutual
interest would sanction or require. Were the French to assume any authority
inconsistent with the purest independence, it would be the signal for their
destruction. We sought their aid—and we sought it as we had assurance we
should obtain it—as auxiliaries in war, and allies in peace. Were the French
to come as invaders or enemies, uninvited by the wishes of the people, I
should oppose them to the utmost of my strength. Yes! my countrymen, I
should advise you to meet them upon the beach with a sword in one hand

and a torch in the other. I would meet them with all the destructive fury of war. I would animate my countrymen to immolate them in their boats, before they had contaminated the soil of my country. If they succeeded in landing, and we were forced to retire before superior discipline, I would dispute every inch of ground, burn every blade of grass, and my last entrenchment of liberty should be the grave. What I could not do myself, if I should fall, I should leave as a last charge to my countrymen to accomplish; because I should feel conscious that life, any more than death, is unprofitable when a foreign nation holds my country in subjection.

' But it was not as enemies that the succours of France were to land. I looked, indeed, for the assistance of France; but I wished to prove to France and to the world that Irishmen deserved to be assisted—that they were indignant at slavery, and ready to assert the independence and liberty of their country. I wished to procure for my country the guarantee which Washington procured for America—and to procure an aid which, by its example, would be as important as its valour; disciplined, gallant, pregnant with science and experience; that of a people who would perceive the good and polish the rough points of our character. They would come to us as strangers, and leave us as friends, after sharing in our perils and elevating our destiny. These were my objects; not to receive new taskmasters, but to expel old tyrants. It was for these ends I sought aid from France; because France, even as an enemy, could not be more implacable than the enemy already in the bosom of my country.'

[Here he was interrupted by the court.]

' I have been charged with that importance in the emancipation of my country as to be considered the keystone of the combination of Irishmen, or, as your lordship expressed it, " the life and blood of the conspiracy." You do honour me over much; you have given to the subaltern all the credit of a superior. There are men engaged in this conspiracy who are not only superior to me, but even to your own conceptions of yourself, my lord,—men before the splendour of whose genius and virtues I should bow with respectful deference, and who would think themselves disgraced by shaking your blood-stained hand.'

[Here he was again interrupted.]

' What, my lord, shall you tell me, on the passage to the scaffold, which that tyranny (of which you are only the intermediary executioner) has erected for my murder, that I am accountable for all the blood that has been and will be shed in this struggle of the oppressed against the oppressor—shall you tell me this, and must I be so very a slave as not to repel it? I do not fear to approach the Omnipotent Judge to answer for the conduct of my whole life; and am I to be appalled and falsified by a mere remnant of mortality here? By you, too, although if it were possible to collect all the innocent blood that you have shed in your unhallowed ministry in one great reservoir, your lordship might swim in it.'

[Here the judge interfered further.]

' Let no man dare, when I am dead, to charge me with dishonour; let no man attaint my memory by believing that I could have engaged in any cause but that of my country's liberty and independence; or that I could have become the pliant minion of power in the oppression and misery of my country. The proclamation of the Provisional Government speaks for our views; no inference can be tortured from it to countenance barbarity or debasement at home, or subjection, humiliation or treachery from abroad. I would not have submitted to a foreign oppressor, for the same reason that I would resist the foreign and domestic oppressor. In the dignity of freedom, I would have fought upon the threshold of my country, and its enemy should enter only by passing over my lifeless corpse. And am I, who lived but for my country, and who have subjected myself to the dangers of the jealous and watchful oppressor, and the bondage of the grave, only to give my countrymen their rights, and my country her independence,—am I to be loaded with calumny, and not suffered to resent it? No; God forbid!'

[Here Lord Norbury told Mr. Emmet that his sentiments and language disgraced his family and his education, but more particularly his father, Dr. Emmet, who was a man, if alive, that would not countenance such opinions. To which Mr. Emmet replied.]

'If the spirits of the illustrious dead participate in the concerns and cares of those who were dear to them in this transitory life, oh! ever dear and venerated shade of my departed father, look down with scrutiny upon the conduct of your suffering son, and see if I have, even for a moment, deviated from those principles of morality and patriotism which it was your care to instil into my youthful mind, and for which I am now about to offer up my life. My lords, you are impatient for the sacrifice. The blood which you seek is not congealed by the artificial terrors which surround your victim—it circulates warmly and unruffled through the channels which God created for noble purposes, but which you are now bent to destroy, for purposes so grievous that they cry to heaven. Be yet patient! I have but a few more words to say—I am going to my cold and silent grave—my lamp of life is nearly extinguished—my race is run—the grave opens to receive me, and I sink into its bosom. I have but one request to ask at my departure from this world: it is—THE CHARITY OF ITS SILENCE. Let no man write my epitaph; for as no man who knows my motives dare now vindicate them, let not prejudice or ignorance asperse them. Let them and me rest in obscurity and peace, and my tomb remain uninscribed, and my memory in oblivion, until other times and other men can do justice to my character. When my country takes her place among the nations of the earth, *then, and not till then,* let my epitaph be written. I have done.'

THE PRISONER IN THE TOWER

Contemporary statement by Mrs. Alice Stopford Green, the historian.

Sir Roger Casement was taken prisoner on April 21st, and brought direct to London. His two cousins, who had been brought up with him as sisters, and were his nearest relations in Europe, made application to see him. They also offered to supply any necessaries of clothing that might be required. Mrs. Green also applied to see him as an old friend. On May 1st Mr. Gavin Duffy, at the wish of Sir Roger's cousins, sent a letter by hand to the Tower, enclosed to the Governor, with an offer of advising him as to his defence. No answer was received to any of these applications, and none of them was mentioned to Sir Roger, neither the offer of clothes nor the offer of legal advice. Sir Roger knew of only one solicitor in London to whom he had applied for legal help at an earlier date, and had been decisively refused. This was all that reached him from the outer world. Meanwhile stories were circulated in the most influential quarters that Sir Roger had turned ' King's evidence ', and had made ' full confession ', and that he had with the calmest deliberation decided to make no defence.

Mr. Gavan Duffy, having had no answer to his application, went to the War Office on May 9th or 10th, and was given leave to visit the prisoner, who had not been informed of his coming or his purpose. Mr. Duffy brought back the list of necessary clothing he required, as not a single article had been furnished, and he remained in the same clothes and boots, which had been drenched and hardened with sea water nearly three weeks before. The cousins immediately sent to the War Office an essential change of garments. After repeated applications they were allowed to see him on May 11th. The clothes had not been delivered to him. They were only then handed out, and the visit was deferred until the prisoner had time to dress in clean garments. Thus he only received a change of clothes in three weeks less one day after his capture, and was in the same clothes in which he had travelled in the submarine.

Mrs. Green's application to see him had been ignored throughout.

The method of procedure had increased the difficulties of defence. The Government preparation was extended through three weeks, in which time no one had access to the prisoner except police officials. Conflicting rumours were spread as to what the charge would be. The charge was finally shown to the solicitor for the defence on May 12th, and the trial was to open on the 15th. There were no means whatever in hand for expenses. Very little time was left to confer with the few friends within immediate reach, and to engage help. A violent prejudice overcame the right tradition of the Bar that every accused person should have the opportunity of a perfectly fair trial with the necessary legal aid. The solicitor, to whom the prisoner applied, refused to act. The second solicitor had his name struck off the list of his firm, and underwent considerable loss and difficulty. It has been found impossible so far to obtain a leading counsel. The case is one that shows the extraordinary disadvantage at which a poor man stands, if accused of crime; and also the dangerous effect of popular clamo"

BIBLIOGRAPHY

History of the Irish Volunteers, by Bulmer Hobson.

John Redmond's Last Years, by Stephen Gwynn.

From Three Yachts, by Conor O'Brien.

Annals of an Active Life, by Sir Nevil Macready.

Secret History of the Irish Volunteers, by The O'Rahilly.

Recollections of the Irish War, by Darrell Figgis.

Last Changes, Last Chances, by H. W. Nevinson.

Field Marshal Sir Henry Wilson : his Life and Diaries, by Major-General C. E. Callwell.

The Crime Against Europe. A possible outcome of the War of 1914, by Sir Roger Casement. 1915. (The Celtic Press, Philadelphia, U.S.A.).

The Crime Against Ireland and How the War may Right it, by Sir Roger Casement.

Ireland, Germany and the Freedom of the Seas. A possible outcome of the War of 1914, by Sir Roger Casement, 1914. (Irish Press Bureau, New York and Philadelphia, Sept. 1, 1914).

The Causes of the War and the Foundations of Peace. The Keeper of the Seas, by Sir Roger Casement. (Jos. C. Hubers Verlag, Diessen vor München, 1915).

Diaries of Sir Roger Casement : His Mission to Germany and the Findlay Affair, edited by Dr. Charles E. Curry. 1922. (Arche Publishing Co., Munich, Germany).

Some Poems of Roger Casement, with an introduction by Gertrude Parry. 1918. (Talbot Press, Dublin).

Irland, Deutschland und die Freiheit der Meere, und andere Aufsätze, by Sir Roger Casement. (Jos. C. Hubers Verlag, Diessen vor München).

Casement in Deutschland, by Dr. Franz Rothenfelder. (Augsburg, 1917. Verlag Gebruder Reichel).

The Life and Death of Roger Casement, by Denis Gwynn. 1930. (Jonathan Cape, London).

Sir Roger Casement, by L. G. Redmond-Howard. 1916. (Hodges, Figgis & Co., Dublin).

Vindication of Roger Casement, by Padraic Colum. (*Current History*, September, 1931).

Casement, by F. Swinnerton.

Casement's Last Adventure, by Robert Monteith. 1932. (Privately printed in America).

Gun-Running for Casement, by Karl Spindler. 1921. (English translation : W. Collins, Sons & Co., London).

The Mystery of the Casement Ship, with authentic documents, by Karl Splindler. (Kribe Verlag, Berlin).

Trial of Roger Casement, edited by G. H. Knott. 1917. (Notable British Trials Series : William Hodge & Co., London).

The Forged Casement Diaries, by William J. Maloney, M.D., LL.D. (The Talbot Press Limited, Dublin).

Roger Casement, by Geoffrey de C. Parmiter. (Arthur Barker, Ltd., London).